Forever in Our Hearts

2/05

Sr. Mary Jean Horne $10.00

Dear Sister Mary Jean,
    Thank you for all you
did for the St. Vincent's
Girls. God bless you,
                    Nita Smith

by

Nita Mondoñedo Smith

B
SMI

PublishAmerica
Baltimore

First printing

ISBN: 1-4137-3850-8
PUBLISHED BY PUBLISHAMERICA, LLLP
www.publishamerica.com
Baltimore

Printed in the United States of America

Acknowledgments

I cannot thank the alumnae of St. Vincent's and St. Rose's enough for their contributions and encouragement in this endeavor.

My greatest debt of gratitude is owed to my sister, Mattie Walker, who lives in Clearlake, California. She encouraged me for several years to "plow on" when I procrastinated. She threatened to write her version of the experience, poles apart from mine, if I did not complete this work. When I had a severe hand injury, she continued the process by typing the early chapters.

Thanks to my children, Kelly, Kristina and Kristofer Heidler, now grown adults, who were the unfortunate "victims" and the unknowing "recipients" of my experiences at St. Vincent's. Despite their own impoverished upbringing, my three heroes transcended many obstacles and achieved much, personally and professionally.

Un millón de grácias to Mary Bullard and Rosalie V.Gregory for dotting my *I*s, for crossing my *T*s and for making sense of my often scrambled thoughts and words in writing this book. I express the same debt of gratitude for the drills in English grammar, punctuation, and diagraming of sentences to the Holy Cross Sisters of St. Peter's and the former St. Patrick's Academy, and to the teaching Sisters of Notre Dame deNamur of the former St. Aloysius School, in Washington, D.C. Thanks, Jack, in Shepherdstown, WV.

This work could not have been finished without the help and understanding of my husband, Gene Smith, who grew up at the other end of the Potomac River. He respects the "orphan" in me, and proves every day that love given proliferates and empowers.

Thanks to the Daughters of Charity at the Motherhouse and the staff at the Archives at Emmitsburg, Maryland and at the St. Louise House in Albany, New York. and especially to Sister Mary of St. Catherine's in Emmitsburg, who never ceases to love, nurture and fret about the many subject women, the "St. Vincent girls."

Table of Contents

Part Two: A Quick Escape

Part Three: Going Back Home

Foreword

D.C.'s hotter than hell in the summer. The word "muggy" must be a Washington word, just another one of those cutesy, polite words we use to disguise what we really mean. We use them all the time for the weather. The all-knowing meteorologists get away with saying it's "uncomfortably warm" or "a little bit humid" for describing a day that should be called "damned near sizzling," or more precisely, "a day to fry eggs on Constitution Avenue." They are simply understatements.

People do have different views on things—things that are the same, experienced at the same time, and under the same circumstances. The same colored stones inside a child's kaleidoscope will be viewed differently with every turn of the viewer. Emphatically, things are seen differently. When some horrible event occurs, some people call it a catastrophe while others perceive it as "fate." And there are those cock-eyed optimists that can see some good come out of a tragedy. It's all about one's perspective.

And so it was viewed differently—living at St. Vincent's in that huge institution, run by the Daughters of Charity, separated from our families.

From my perspective, it felt like a "boarding school." That's what I called it, when school friends asked me about my home. I deluded myself into thinking it was like a typical boarding school for girls. I always thought that boarding schools were for very spoiled children whose parents had too much money and too little time for them.

Jamie, who was my best friend in high school, can always be counted on to be completely objective and accurate. She never hesitates to tell friends: *"I grew up in an orphanage."* My sister, Magdalina, who hated every day at St. Vincent's, and was quite verbal and expressive of this fact, describes it this way:*"It was just like a jail."*

The same era. The same circumstances. We all viewed it differently. But Jamie was right—technically, it was an orphanage. It was St. Vincent's Home and School at Fourth and Edgewood Streets, on a hill overlooking Union Station in Northeast Washington, D.C.

There are several personal accounts related to our dysfunctional family that were shared only with my sister, Magdalina. But much of what happened to us may be typical of what happened to many of the girls who lived at St. Vincent's throughout the generations of its 143-year-old history.

Many of the names of the Sisters and the girls have been changed to assure privacy. They are, even as adult women, reticent about sharing the details and events of their childhood at St. Vincent's. Others have eagerly provided me with stories of their experiences.

My intention is not to offend anyone by the use of these stories but rather to provide a holistic account of the actual experience of living at St. Vincent's in the City of Washington during those times. It is a testament to the loving care we received by the Daughters of Charity.

My story begins when I first entered St. Vincent's in the summer of 1952. It is my perspective of life at St. Vincent's and the environs. It is my best recollection of the events that occurred, from 1952 until the summer of 1964, when I graduated from high school. Admittedly, the views are rather biased and absent of extensive historical research of the home and of the era. Forgive me. The order of the stories may be somewhat confusing. So were the times.

We had common bonds. We were very much like biological sisters—all 100 of us—sharing the same food and being cared for together, patiently and not so patiently struggling and coping with the unjust situations that originally placed us under the care of the Daughters of Charity at St. Vincent's. Then, facing the world together, when we went out to school each day we assimilated ourselves into society.

Together, the girls of St. Vincent's learned about God, His generosity, His mercy and His forgiveness. We learned to live together and share in a community. We learned to graciously accept His blessings through the kindness bestowed upon us by the Sisters.

At times we were intolerable little waifs and they loved us despite our behavior. They were patient, kind, wise and forgiving. Some of us were rescued from a tragic life on the streets. All of us were directed on the path toward becoming respectable, contributing members of the community.

Sister Serena Branson, who died in July 2003, set forth a philosophy for the treatment of the dependent girls of St. Vincent's which was presented in her dissertation for a Master's Degree in Social Work from Catholic University. This philosophy was respected and remained in effect from the time she was Superior of St. Vincent's in 1946 until the facility was closed down in 1968.

She directed that: *"This institution will continue to do its part in bringing to these children that heritage which is their birthright, the knowledge and love of Jesus Christ, who is the author of their being and their last end."* How could their noble mission fail with such an astounding belief!

The title of this memoir, *Forever in our Hearts,* is the response to a short prayer that Sister Bernard woke us with each morning. She would enthusiastically turn on the overhead fluorescent lights and say *"Live Jesus!"* Her 20 high school girls responded *"Forever in our Hearts."*

In the summer of 1999 Magdalina, Jamie and I visited Sister Alma who now lives in Albany, New York. The drive from the Washington, D.C. area gave the three of us lots of time to reminisce about the many memories we cherish about our childhood at St. Vincent's. We all agreed that Sister Alma's love and sense of humor brightened many of our dark days of loneliness and difficult times. She was truly the mother we did not have.

Listening to an oldies station, and singing along with the radio on the trip to Albany evoked many wonderful times. It helped Jamie and I to relate for Magdalina some of the stories of our years in the high school group with Sister Bernard. Since she was not at St. Vincent's for her high school years, she was not familiar with the prayer.

9

Magdalina noticed that Jamie and I were saying the prayer differently. Again, a perspective. More likely, however, there was an "audiological defect" on someone's part!

My rendition of the prayer was, "LIFT Jesus;" Jamie said, "LIVE Jesus." After years of saying this prayer early at the beginning of each day, we both insisted we were right. We decided that when we got to Albany we would ask Sister Alma to confirm the correct wording of the prayer.

The dispute was handled with Sister's usual wisdom and humor. The words are "Live Jesus," Sister Alma said, "Juanita, no wonder life was so hard for you at times." Then demonstrating with both hands, she bent her knees, pushed heavenward with a grunt and said,"You were literally trying to LIFT Jesus up every single morning. That's a tall order!"

The Sisters used to refer to their "missions in Bolivia," projects in which Daughters of Charity, the order founded by St. Vincent dePaul, risked their lives to bring food and clothing and the word of God to the people of that country. The Sisters at St. Vincent's would listen to these missionary stories wistfully, feeling their assignments were less glamorous, perhaps less appreciated.

But, we were their mission! They did not have to travel through the treacherous Andes to find purpose. We ragged urchins, with boundless physical needs and demands on their time and patience, were the objects of their dedication in the name of God. In the heart of the Nation's Capitol, we were their mission.

This book is dedicated to those noble Sisters, in appreciation for the love and kindness bestowed upon all of the girls who lived at St. Vincent's.

Part One:
A Grand Entrance

From the Beginning

"Love you Maggie. Love you Neet-neet. Now say your prayers and get into bed. Your daddy's coming to see you girls tomorrow," Aunt Edna said. Her belly was so swollen, she couldn't kneel down on the floor with us to say our prayers. Uncle Braulio said she swallowed a watermelon seed.

My sister Maggie and I felt loved. We were very cozy in our roomy two-story row house on South Carolina Avenue in Capitol Hill. We loved the Rillon family. We were excited about the next day's adventures with our father and found it hard to sleep that night.

It had been a long day filled with some of our typical activities for a Sunday. Our cousins Janice and Raymond Rillon had taken us to the children's Mass at St. Peter's Church. They gave in to our dirty little Sunday morning habit—that of letting us take the money that was intended for the church collection to buy records from the little toy store near the Eastern Market on Pennsylvania Avenue. We couldn't resist the bright yellow 78-speed records, so we bought *Little Red Caboose*. Aunt Edna would be angry with us.

It had happened before. Ray had a real passion for toy trains and he had actually bought parts for his Lionel layout with the money intended for the Sunday collection basket too. But he knew how to handle his mom and she would then go easy on Maggie and me.

Usually, we just sat around in the afternoon at home, looking at the *Washington Post* from cover to cover, spending extra time pouring through the travel section and the funnies. There were always two sets of comics in the Sunday paper. Uncle Braulio and his friend from his office at Health, Education and Welfare, went to the clay courts nearby to play tennis.

That evening after dinner we had ice cream with the Songco family—Aunt Bea, who was Aunt Edna's older sister, Uncle Dempsey and our cousins, Pat, David, Gracie Lou, Betty Bea and Jeanine. They just lived at the other end of South Carolina Avenue on the same block.

Uncle Dempsey played his steel guitar. He let us go through his collection of black-and-white photos he had developed himself. Aunt Bea listened to my story about being locked in the classroom with another kindergartener.

"Did you have your dog tag around your neck, Sweetie Neetie?"

I told Aunt Bea she was silly and, "No one ever brings their dog tags to school!" She was happy that the janitor rescued us before we were even missed and before Aunt Edna went bonkers. We all listened to Grannie's predictions that she read, looking closely at the coffee grinds left in Aunt Bea's cup.

"Looks like no more babies, Beatrice." She twisted her head and adjusted her glasses every which way to focus on the grinds in the cup. " Five's enough for any woman!"

When Grannie tired of this game, she conned one of the older boys into getting some of her "vitamins" from the kitchen—a big brown glass bottle of National Bo. Our oldest cousin, Pat, had probably gotten the beer from the liquor store around the corner, with Grannie going through her usual routine. She would just endorse her Social Security check and write you a note for permission to buy her brew. The clerk would cash her monthly check, give you the change, all in five-dollar bills, and send you on your way home with her beer.

We caught lightning bugs in one of Grannie's beer bottles as we walked back home. Aunt Bea's was just down at the other side of South Carolina Avenue, so there was no rush to get home. We saw the gas lamps go on that lit up our street.

The watermelon man had just passed our house, Number "306," his horse-drawn cart almost emptied of his day's stock of the ripest, plumpest produce in Southeast. We heard his familiar chant, never knowing it would be our last time to sing along with him, placing our hands over our mouths, pretending to be shocked at the words:

14

"Watermelon, watermelon, ripe to the rind,
If you don't like it you can kiss mah b'hind."

The milkman would be around too in just a few hours to leave a quart of milk for our morning Corn Flakes. Uncle Tashio would dump the cream into his coffee cup, saving a little for his older brother, Braulio. The cream filled the top fourth of the glass milk bottle, the part that had the happy face shape. Then he would give us a sip of his hot steaming coffee and promise to bring home a Hershey bar if we got up off his lap so he could go to work. We liked bribes. And we knew he'd remember the Hershey bar because a Rillon's promise was as good as gold.

The next day, June 16, 1952, finally rolled around. It was different. Our father came and took us across town. We were used to riding with him in his taxicab so we were not too concerned that we did not recognize the streets he traveled and where we were going. Of course we thought he would bring us back to Aunt Edna's in the evening.

Dad passed the Capitol and headed north on North Capitol Street then turned onto Rhode Island Avenue. Nothing looked familiar.

"You girls are going to live somewhere else, somewhere completely different from your Aunt Edna's house."

We knew that Uncle Braulio's brother Lakay died a few months before this took place. We missed seeing him every night. It was wonderful to have so many uncles living with us and to have an aunt and uncle and lots of cousins living right on the same block. We did not understand how emotionally attached everyone was to Uncle Lakay. But we did feel that everything changed when Uncle Lakay died.

"The Rillon family is very sad right now because of the death of Lakay. Your Aunt Edna is going to have a baby and it is time for you two to be with more children your own age. You are going to be living at the big home called St. Vincent's," Dad assured us.

We listened to him but continued to play games in the back seat of his Chevy taxicab. His dark brown bony fingers tightened on the steering wheel. He looked straight ahead when he talked.

"Your Aunt Gracie lived at this place before she got married. You will see. By and by you will like it there very much."

Still the information did not really sink in and we just sat back and enjoyed the ride.

The trip to St. Vincent's took about 25 minutes. The first encounter with the new "Home" was driving up the steep hill and parking in the circular driveway in front of the building. We got out of the car and climbed the steep stairs that looked like the marble steps on so many of the Washington Government buildings. We were greeted at the portico by Sister Elizabeth, who walked with us up another flight of stairs, then entered the building through a set of double doors made of wood.

Inside was a large foyer where another nun had us leave our box of clothing. We did not have a suitcase because we had never taken a vacation before and never owned one. Walking off to the right of the foyer, the nun paraded us through a pleasant-looking parlor with elongated windows trimmed in heavy wood. We were impressed with the size of the room. It had at least three sofas, half a dozen armchairs with small side tables and lamps in attractive groupings throughout the parlor.

Maggie jumped on one of the sofas, as if to test the springs. It was apparent Sister did not approve of this. She did not scold her, just took both her hands and led Maggie back through the foyer and into another room — the office.

There were not enough chairs in the office for all of us so she told Dad to sit and she took her seat behind the desk by the window. It was a busy looking place with papers and books stacked everywhere. There were lots of photographs of teenage girls on the walls, their names written in fancy writing. One frame had a collage of photographs and calligraphy writing under each to identify the girl. The photographs all had been finished with that special hand coloring process that makes your cheeks look rosy as though rouge had been applied. I could not help staring at one of the photographs in particular . The script writing said, "May Winkler." She had dark hair, dark eyes, a beautiful pinkish complexion and a small scarf tied around her neck, the ends of the silk scarf very fashionably angled to one side.

After Sister Elizabeth finished completing some paperwork for Dad to sign, a teenage girl appeared to help carry our box of clothes to our dormitory. This girl was pretty too, but she was not May Winkler. We liked her penny loafers with the shiny dimes in the leather slots. We finally said goodbye to Dad and walked off with the teenage girl.

Maggie was holding my hand as tight as a tourniquet and didn't let go until another Sister, Sister Cecilia, brought us on the elevator up to Group One on the third floor. Sister Cecilia was the Superior and she scared us. We did not say a word even when she spoke to us. She brought us to Miss Nora, a kind white-haired woman, who would be our main caretaker for the next several years.

The rest of the day was a blur of activity, from going out to "The Grove"—the backyard—to the swimming pool and back up to Group One to get ready for dinner.

The evening ritual was strange at this new place—20 little girls all about five or six years old, hair in plastic curlers, squeaky clean from the bathtubs, dressed in cotton nightgowns, kneeling around a small table covered with a white eyelet cloth, topped with a wooden crucifix. We stared as they recited.

"Jesus hanging on the cross, tell me was it I?
I see those great big teardrops, Lord. Did I make you cry?
I have been a naughty child, naughty as can be.
Now I am so sorry, Lord, won't you pardon me."

They all bowed their heads when they said the word *Jesus*. Then there was a song the little girls sang as they remained on their knees. We listened and stared some more.

"Goodnight sweet Jesus. Guard us in sleep.
Our souls and bodies, in thy love keep.
Waking or sleeping, keep us in sight.
Dear Savior gentle, goodnight, goodnight!"

Each little girl pulled her chenille bedspread down, folded it over neatly at the foot of her bed, got into her own bed. The little nun whose name was Sister Margaret, went into her room, her *cell*, and shut the door. It was quiet. We could see shadows on the ceiling that came from the light in her cell. We could tell she was reading because you could hear the turning of pages of a book in the still night.

It was hard to sleep. The building was so huge, the ceilings were so high, and the sheets on the iron beds were so white and starchy. We were not supposed to talk until morning. It was so lonely, even with the other 18 little girls in the dormitory and so very, very strange. We missed Aunt Edna. We missed being tucked in and we missed her big bear hugs and kisses. It was so still. It was such a long time ago. At six years old, I thought it was truly the end of the world.

We knew that our Aunt Grace had lived at St. Vincent's when she was just a teenager. Dad seemed to think that if it were "good enough for your Aunt Gracie," that it should be good enough for us.

Aunt Grace loved men in uniform, like everyone else in her high school group. Her brother, Jimmy Helphenstine, came to see her at St. Vincent's, decked out in his crisp Merchant Marines uniform, and surely caused a lot of ogling from the "boy crazy" high school girls peeking out the upstairs windows to get a better view of a "real man on campus."

At sixteen, Aunt Grace ran away with Joe Dioso, a man much older than herself who was in the Navy. She admitted that she had to get out of St. Vincent's because "those nuns made us pray all the time." Somehow, just because Aunt Grace had lived there once, this never seemed to be a good enough reason to put us there, but Dad had a lot of faith in the work of the "good nuns."

Dad was familiar with the Daughters of Charity from Providence Hospital, just across the street from St. Peter's and confirmed that the "bird wing" sisters, half ridiculing the "habit," the clothing of the Daughters of Charity, were just as kind as the "daisy" sisters, referring to the habit of the Sisters of Holy Cross.

He thought all nuns were an odd lot, not wanting to get married and to have a husband, children or a home. But he entrusted us to their care. And this was our new home.

Dad came every Sunday at one o'clock and took us out. We would visit with him at the house where he worked on Ashmead Place. We'd have dinner with him there or go out to eat, then head back to arrive at St. Vincent's by five thirty.

When about two months had gone by, Sister let Dad pick us up a little earlier so that we could visit Aunt Edna. She had given birth to a new baby. She named him *Ralph Michael*. We were happy to see our cousins Janice and Ray after such a long separation.

18

"The baby cries all night long," they told us. They wished that we would come back. They would gladly send Ralphie back to the hospital. We missed them, too.

We missed the old house on Capitol Hill as well. The Rillons had moved to Oxon Run Hills in Maryland and bought a new house—a brick duplex. The red-brick house was smaller, much smaller. They had to give half of their old furniture to the junk man, including my favorite oak dining room table with the big claw feet. They used the old kitchen table in their new dining room. Uncle Braulio now had to drive to his office at H.E.W. It was too far to walk. He was so tired after work he didn't play tennis on the weekends anymore. He said he hated the traffic going over the Sousa Bridge.

Uncle Tashio, who drove a taxicab all day in the District, now had to travel from Maryland just to get to work. He even had to buy two license plates for his cab—one for the District and one for the State of Maryland.

Aunt Edna was trying to help everyone with the new transition. She sat us all down and, like a coach for a football game, she told us that nothing stays the same. All things change for the better. Just like they say at a funeral when they are standing over the dead body, Aunt Edna assured us that we were all "in a better place." This was hard to swallow.

She even talked about Maggie and me having a swimming pool in the backyard at St. Vincent's, to the envy of Janice and Ray. We didn't think we were in a better place. We were not that crazy about the swimming pool either. But no one asked us for our opinion!

High on a Hill

Fourth and Edgewood Streets, Northeast, Washington 17, D.C. The address had a certain touch of class to it for the 1950s. The folks in the working-class neighborhood near Catholic University in Washington, D.C. surrounding the 19-acre parcel of partly wooded land on the hill, knew very little about the girls, as many as 150 residents at any given time, ranging in age from 5 or 6 years old, up to 18, who called St. Vincent's their home.

Administered through Catholic Charities and the Daughters of Charity, St. Vincent's Home had actually included a school in the early years. During World War II and for a time after, St. Vincent's had also been used as a residence for women who worked at federal agencies in Washington, D.C.

By the time we arrived in 1952, the school operation was discontinued, and everyone was sent out to local schools, primarily Catholic schools in the immediate neighborhood. Because Aunt Edna had agreed to watch my sister Maggie—"MM"—every day after her morning kindergarten session, we were allowed to cross the city every day on Capitol Transit to attend St. Peter's School in Capitol Hill, accompanied by a sixth grade girl from St. Vincent's.

This would be considered taboo in the new millennium—the idea of children five and six years old using public transportation and transferring on buses in downtown Washington, D.C. Later, I continued on at St. Peter's and MM walked to St. Martin's with several other girls her age and one older girl who supervised them while they walked to school. St. Martin's was the closest parish school to St. Vincent's, located at North Capitol Street and Rhode Island Avenue.

Everything at St. Vincent's was big. First, there was "the hill" which meandered up from the intersection at Fourth and Edgewood Streets, Northeast to the actual five-story building. Next, there was the name "St. Vincent's Home and School" which stretched out on a four-foot wide sign placed midway up the big hill leading to the circular driveway at the front door of St. Vincent's.

The entrance way was intimidating with its formal façade—a welcome portico with its high set of marble stairs, flanked on either side by three-foot cement urns. Once inside the huge set of double doors, the building seemed to grow larger still. The ceilings were about 10 feet high and, although the dear nuns were about average height, they seemed almost as high as those mighty ceilings, their starched white headdress, the "cornette," like big birds pointing their wings up to the sky in prayer.

The navy blue dress, the "habit," with the bell-shaped open sleeves, added to the Sisters' resemblance to a bird. The thick cord knotted around their waist was the only thing that anchored them so they didn't fly off. Despite its likeness to a bird, the habit gave an extremely dignified appearance to any Sister who was blessed with a vocation in the Daughters of Charity.

Life at St. Vincent's was a great adventure for a little "tomboy." St. Vincent's Home offered as many opportunities to get in trouble outdoors as well as inside the huge building.

Outside there were gigantic oak, pear, apple and mulberry trees, and a couple of weeping willow trees whose sweeping, whip-like branches dipped down into a creek. Just like Tarzan swinging through the jungle, we would beat our chest and yell, and swing over the creek into the woods that surrounded the property.

Our backyard was called "the Grove." It had two sets of swings, monkey bars, a sliding board, see-saws, a sandbox and an almost Olympic-size swimming pool with a diving and sliding board. The pool was enclosed by a chain-link fence, topped by a foot of barbed wire. There was a little brick utility building, which we climbed to get a better view of the swimming pool.

The focal point of the Grove was the Lourdes Grotto—a life-size stone and mortar altar and statues of Our Lady and Bernadette, surrounded by miniature rose bushes and other greenery along the stone pathway leading up to the altar.

It was great place to pretend you were saying or attending Mass. Sometimes for Communion we would use the wafer-type fish that Hartz Mountain made for goldfish. They were thin and very authentic, with very little taste. But Necco wafers were more delicious as candy hosts. Hope Baza freaked out one time when she received a black wafer, randomly chosen of course. She thought it meant that she was going to hell.

Smoking was probably one of the things that could send you to hell. Very few girls tried smoking cigarettes. It was simply not worth the hell you'd catch from Sister if she found out. But on one occasion, smoking one of those cigar-like sticks from the bean tree in the backyard was just too tempting. Several of us sat cross-legged on the ground in a circle like Indians smoking a peace pipe. The few matches we had didn't work but that did not stop us from having fun. We'd pass the cigar around and make some wise crack that today would be confused for corny bumper stickers:

Me heap big Injun chief, smokum peace pipe.
LSMFT, Lucky Strike Means Fine Tobacco"
Or:
"So round, so mild, so fully packed!"
Or maybe:
"Luckies taste sour just like Eisenhower
Up in a tower taking a shower!"

For many of us, however, the real highlight of the Grove was the merry-go-round. This is what we called it but a better description would be "the circling iron torture chamber." Looking very much like a huge umbrella minus the canvas, it consisted of a huge center pole of iron and iron bars for umbrella spokes, circled by thick wooden planking and a circular bar for your feet. It could seat at least 10 girls, but we tested its limits and there are photographs that prove it would hold dozens more. The daredevils would take turns sitting on the top of the pole, a cap barely a foot wide, while we twirled and banged the foot bar against the central pole—dangerous for everyone and especially the foolish girl who sat on the top!

Snow blanketed down the steep rolling front hill, icicles glistening as they dripped slowly, like the stalactite and stalagmite crystals we saw when we toured Luray Caverns in Virginia. From December through February our 19-acres on the hill was transformed into a winter wonderland.

The little girls in Groups One and Two would bundle up like Eskimos, dressed in warm woolen mittens, snow suits, calf-high rubber boots and old-fashioned leggings, to go sleigh riding on some old, really old, toboggans, down the steep front hill. It did not matter that there were very few sleds to go around. We took turns, piling two or three girls on the sled at a time.

There were angel shapes to make as you lay on the ground, ice forts to build and snowball battles to fight while you waited to use the slide. Then you might even sneak back inside the house to buy a Coke from the basement Coke machine and use it to make real snow cones outside.

You were supposed to stop the sled inside the gates, not playing in the street beyond the property line, but it was even more fun if you went beyond the gates and onto Edgewood Street. We must have looked like three-headed aliens sleigh-riding down the hill. We were the envy of the immediate neighborhood kids. When it was just too cold to be outside, we would abandon our hill and get warmed up inside. We'd look out the windows in the evening and see the neighborhood kids using our hill.

Icicles hung off the Grotto, off the Blessed Mother and St. Bernadette statues, off the huge evergreen fir trees that surrounded the entire property and most beautifully, off the garage behind the main building. Those hanging daggers could be three or four feet long and as much as three inches in diameter and were extremely dangerous.

Despite the number of times we were told to stay away from the garage, especially when it snowed, it was just too tempting not to snap the ice swords down and use them as weapons to fight off imaginary ice dragons or even some neighborhood thugs trying to use our hill for sleigh riding. Bill Marean, the driver for the Sisters, kept the station wagon in this garage. It was actually warmer outside of the garage, so he would pull the car out of the garage and get us to help him clear off the windows when he had to make a trip in the snow.

Sister Alma's cocoa, made the right way with real milk scalded in a saucepan, the best we'd ever had, awaited us when we finally waddled back indoors and hung up our tons of wet clothing. A snow day usually ended with everyone sitting around the tiny TV, no closer than six feet, as recommended by the manufacturer, watching the Mickey Mouse Club or the Milt Grant Show, if you were in the high school group. Some girls might single off to read or to sit at a card table to do a 1000-piece jigsaw puzzle, already in progress.

Almost anything you did, after a day of playing in the snow, made you feel warm and cozy. This was especially true at Christmas time when looking out at the brightly decorated City of Washington from one of the City's most spectacular vantage points—from the windows on the third floor or from the attic at St. Vincent's. You could not see much of downtown from there, but you did get a magnificent view of the immediate Rhode Island Avenue neighborhood where the present-day Rhode Island Avenue Metro station is located, and a little off in the distance you could see the rail yard at Union Station and the U.S. Capitol building. You could see what looked like a long snake of starry lights and you knew you were looking at Rhode Island Avenue that went from Mt. Ranier, Maryland on one side to downtown D.C. on the other. Life was often beautiful high on our hill.

Most of the girls were placed at St. Vincent's through Catholic Charities, and their parents would pay for their board based on their income. A few were there through D.C. Public Welfare. Most of the girls were Catholics, with a very small percentage of girls who had not been baptized.

Our situation was atypical. Our Dad, Felipe Estifano Mondoñedo, had joined the U.S. Navy when he was just a teenager in the Philippines. As logistically incredible as it may sound, Dad served in both World Wars I and II. He stared for months at a billboard sign that promised

"Join the Navy—See the World!"

He found a recruiting station in Manila, enlisted and never looked back. He became a U.S. citizen several years after he returned from his tour of duty in the U.S. Navy. Between World Wars I and II Dad had all kinds of odd jobs including running a restaurant in Baltimore, Maryland.

In the 1950s he worked as a valet and chauffeur for a retired military officer. When he was not working for Major Davis B. Wills, Dad drove a taxicab. There were several Filipina girls at St. Vincent's with a father from the Philippines. They also drove taxicabs, Bell cabs, as a matter of fact.

Having such employment provided Dad with lots of benefits— transportation, free housing, a regular paycheck, no bills other than ongoing maintenance for his cab and he actually paid for us to be at St. Vincent's. So compared to the average girl who was placed there, Sister considered us "privileged characters."

Being a privileged character was a label to be proud of for lots of reasons when Sister pointed her bony finger at you for doing something wrong or something right. Nuns were noted for intimidating little children in those days just with a stare. And far more frightening than a stare, a pointed finger, especially a pointed finger poking at your shoulder, was a much bigger threat than any words could be.

The parents of the other girls were not really "lowlifes" or "welfare bums." They were just ordinary people with ordinary jobs. They just seemed to have too many bills and too many children. Many of the families had been split up by the death of one parent or the other, perhaps mental illness which resulted in the institutionaliza- tion of a parent, divorce or alcohol or all of the above. In those days, men were rarely given custody of their children after a separation, divorce or death of a spouse.

Institutions, or orphanages, like St. Vincent's, were full of non- orphaned girls until they turned 18, or until they were adopted. Sometimes their father remarried and could provide a more traditional home for their daughters.

Most of the other parents did not have cars and relied on public transportation to pick up their daughters for a visit home. But Dad had wheels. So we always left on Sunday afternoon to go home with him for a few hours, and occasionally we were allowed to go home for an overnight stay. Dad picked us up at school every Thursday afternoon, his day off. Then he brought us back to St. Vincent's, usually after a quick stop at the White Tower on Rhode Island Avenue, for a hamburger and French fries.

Bell Cab #147 was a familiar sight on the back driveway near the swimming pool. The girls would all come rushing out to see him when we pulled up. At five feet, four inches tall, he was probably the shortest, and the only brown man, they had ever seen. He always wore a hat, straw in the summer, and a Hawaiian-looking shirt. They called Dad *Ponce Pons* just like the little Hawaiian guy from the show *Hawaiian Eye*. Sometimes they called him "string bean."

Sister had given Dad blanket permission to let our friends hop in the cab and go for a quick ride. He would pile as many girls as could fit in the cab, no seat belts required in those days, flip his Off Duty/On Call sign to Off Duty, and drive out the back gate. The girls would take turns filling in the taxicab "manifest," being sure to put in the date, destination, zones traveled and the fare. Then he would take us around the block and in through the back gate and return to the Grove.

Dad had stories of famous politicians and movie stars he had picked up in the cab. He picked up Danny Kaye, the actor, who hailed Dad in front of the Mayflower Hotel. He'd also tell the girls about the different weapons he kept in the car to protect himself. A Billy club. A hammer. A beer bottle. His wit.

Once he drove Senator John Kennedy and his beautiful wife from their house in Georgetown to a shop on M Street and Wisconsin Avenue, not a long walk but maybe too far in high heels. He retold this story often, remembering that Mrs. Kennedy was a real "hubba hubba" babe, and Mr. Kennedy was a "cheapskate," because he did not leave him a tip. Dad said he would never pick him up again and his opinion about Mr. Kennedy being cheap did not change, not even after John Kennedy became President.

Evidence of politics is everywhere in Washington, D.C. Politicians and celebrities are everywhere, even out on the streets hailing their own cabs. And everyone has definitive political opinions, from the Congressman grabbing lunch at a hot dog stand to the activist who totes around his own grandstand, like an ad for have-soapbox, will-travel.

Growing up in this showground made us develop a healthy respect and awe of the system. We loved America. And at times, it gave us the ability to buck the system when the rhetoric, or whatever that stuff is that gets on your boots, got too thick.

I guess our inclination was to do both—we revered government and were irreverent at the same time. We spent as much time sitting on the steps of the Lincoln Memorial, gazing in amazement at the myriad of memorials dedicated to freedom, as we did kicking off our shoes and splashing around in the Reflecting Pool just for the hell of it!

My sister MM remembers that she was part of a group chosen to visit the White House to meet President Eisenhower. She was scared to death. I have no recollection of this visit at all. Apparently, I was not one of the "chosen ones" to rub elbows with the President. There was also an outing to meet the Ambassadors wives when we were in high school, which Jamie participated in, but for which I was not chosen again.

I do recall very vividly one Christmas being chosen to be a part of a news story at a local TV station. They interviewed about six girls, asking each of us what we wanted Santa Claus to bring us for Christmas. We had been rehearsed by Sister, who had played devil's advocate, getting us ready for almost any question they might ask. We gave very short, polite responses, with no unusual demands to embarrass or perturb the good Sisters, because, as we were told so many times, it was *a* reflection on them.

But we all cringed when the camera was on Donna Jean McCormick. When the interviewer asked her if she had anything special she wanted to say, clutching one of the dolls they had given us, she tilted her head to the side in Shirley Temple style.

"I'm just a little orphan girl and I never had a dolly before. Thank you ever so much!"

The TV station crew loved it. Just the right words to melt the public's hearts at Christmas time. What more could you ask for than this, the true spirit of Christmas and giving.

Well, we gave it to Donna Jean, all right. We let her know just how stupid she was to embarrass us all. The next day was Thursday, laundry day. We put Donna Jean in one of the huge commercial-size Yale laundry carts, shoved the dirty clothes down on top of her and jostled her around as though she were in the *Cuddle-Up* at Glen Echo Park. Finally, we ran the cart down the whole length of the hallway, a good 250 to 300 feet in length.

Sister came running out of the chapel and yelled, "Young ladies!" halting us just as we got to the top of the steps to dump her out. We all got in trouble but it was worth it. Of course "Sister" could have been any one of the eight or more nuns in residence, or any of the many visiting sisters to St. Vincent's.

Too bad Sister saved the girl from the ride of a lifetime down a flight of wide slate steps. But we found lots of other ways to do her in. For a couple of weeks or so, her bed was short-sheeted, and, for some reason, her desserts mysteriously disappeared off her plate every night.

One early day in autumn, Mary Elisabeth Holmes and I were having our usual not-permitted swing from the weeping willow trees that graced the front yard, facing the house, near the Blessed Mother statue, when we decided to go down into the woods and climb the rooftop of the Barber and Ross Company. A man called out over the loudspeaker, warning us to get off. We jumped into the brambles, we were so daring. Our legs and arms were terribly scarred and we were terrified that Sister would find out about us.

We covered our legs from Sister, and tried to act holy from dinnertime until she went to prayers in the evening. Then we cut loose with the moaning and groaning. We were definitely in pain.

We were so bad off we couldn't participate in our favorite game, forbidden by Sister, of sitting on the top of the back of the sofa. One person was designated to pull our legs and let us flop down with a hard thump, squealing as you went down on the rigid green leather sofa.

Most of our waking hours we were in "overdrive," jumping from one activity to the next, bundles of boundless energy, egging one another on, competing for the "Miss Mischievous" award of the group.

But there were quieter, less nervous activities we could involve ourselves in while we were inside the house. There was always a card table or two off to a corner in our living room, with girls seated, playing *Monopoly, Clue, Old Maid, Canasta, Candy Land,* or doing jigsaw or crossword puzzles. This could entertain us for hours. Books, always with a hardback, never a soft cover, were everywhere in those days before computers. We would actually read a book or two in a day, checked out from our library on the first floor or the local public library, then pass it on to the next girl.

MM and I joined a book club through National Geographic. For $1.25 per shipment, plus postage, you would get a small *Around the World* booklet for a particular country that included about 10 to 12 stickers of pictures of different landmarks in that country, that you pasted into the booklet. We collected about 10 different books in over a year, but $1.25 was a lot of money, so we cancelled our membership.

By far, the most mindless sedentary pursuit was watching television. In the baby group, wooden chairs would be lined up in rows, no closer than six feet from the set. This was measured carefully by Sister who, on advise from an expert, knew that this was the safe distance, an established not-to-ruin-your-eyes limit for viewing.

When we lived with Aunt Edna, the coming of the television into American homes was such a new technology. We experienced the constant blow-outs and general lack of programming. We never really relied on our black-and-white TV for entertainment, although my cousin Ray could sit for hours in front of the set, listening to the screechy hum, so loud a dog would fall over from the soundwaves, and staring at the lines of the test patterns on the screen from the broadcast house—those lines that let you know there was nothing being broadcasted!

But at St. Vincent's we watched cartoons on Saturday mornings after we did our Saturday "duty" and every afternoon we always watched *The Mickey Mouse Club,* calling off the names in unison with Jimmie Dodd: Cubby, Karen, Darlene, Bobby, Roy, and our favorite, Annette. We grew older, along with the Mouseketeers, and we watched them mature. We loved Annette in the "Spin and Marty" series.

Our favorite show was always *I Love Lucy.* Our strong identification with the *I Love Lucy* show is having a red-haired, scattered-brained mother, and a father who spoke English with a thick accent. The antics of Lucy and Desi reminded us that our parents, had they stayed together, might have had the same zany but loving relationship.

Even from the time you were in the baby group you were expected to do some kind of housekeeping. There was a chart in each group that listed the daily "duties"—the chores that needed to be done. Sister would assign us our duty that might last a month or two by writing our name on the chart. Each group's duties were about the same but the older you got the more proficiently you were expected to do your duty. Your duty had to be done *before* school so you had to plan your time accordingly.

The "dining room" duty was probably the most dreaded because you had to complete the chores after breakfast and dinner on a school day and for all three meals on the weekends. You had to wash the tables after the meal, sweep the floor and dust the ledges, lights and window sills. Then you had to "weight" the floor.

The weight was an electric buffer machine for shining the floor. This institutional gadget, with the shining brushes under the engine had a long pole that extended to the handles connected to the "ON" lever. It took some skill to get used to and inevitably got us in trouble. When Sister was not around we would take turns riding each other on the weight. There was a delicate balance you maintained. You wanted to scare the girl riding on the weight out of her wits, swinging the weight around furiously. She would hold on to the bar as though she were on a bucking bronco, refushing to let go. But you couldn't get too wild or she would fall off—not your fault! But awfully messy if you got her dress or belt caught in the mechanism. This could make for more work than your duty originally provided you.

The other duties were cleaning the study, living room, locker room/hallway, steps, laundry room, playroom, kitchen, cart and on and on. Some poor girl would end up with the bathroom duty and would clean, with Dutch Cleanser of course, the sinks, hopper, toilets and tubs. She would also have to do the floor.

"Saturday duty" was worst of all. You would have to dust and wet-wash the Venetian blinds, one-by-one. And if you had floors to do during the week, you had to wet-mop, wax and weight the floors on Saturday. Then you had to dry mop them to be sure to get up every little fleck of dust that fell during the process. It was all like being *Cinderella* without going to the ball!

"Do you think Sister Margaret has hair under her cornette?
"No, she shaves it off."
"C'mon, let's peek over at her."
"Not me, I'm not getting in trouble."
"You do it. I dare ya."
"Double dare you!"
"Double dares go first."
"Okay, get me a chair."

So we waited till Sister Maria had gone to prayers, then up I climbed to peak over the cell, just to satisfy everyone's curiosity. The cell was adjacent to Sister Maria's sewing room.

Climb up the chair, onto the locker that stood against the cell where Sister Margaret slept, then over the partition. That's all I had to do and I'd be inside the cell.

With one foot on the wall of the six-foot high partition, the other girls, whispering, urged me to keep going. The chair slipped. Now what? The noise would give me away. I thought, if someone came I'd have to freeze here, straddling the wall of the partition.

To everyone's surprise, however, Sister Margaret coughed out loud but she said nothing. It was way too early for her to take her cornette off and go to sleep, so I climbed down to the locker and jumped to the floor without the help of the chair, and ran outside with the rest of the chickens that put me up to the challenge. Nothing happened right away. The next day after school, however, Sister scolded me for climbing up and peaking over the cell. I was dumfounded. How did she know?

Apparently, Sister Margaret told her she heard several little girls talking, and there was a dark shadow on her wall. Sister Maria concluded that the shadow was created by a girl with black hair. Not a lot of logic here! For a long time after that, I wondered if Sister Maria could have been psychic, or perhaps she just knew me extremely well.

What's in the Attic?

From way up there, you could see the great marble buildings and the presidential memorials of the city of Washington, D.C. Jefferson, Lincoln, Washington. St. Vincent's attic was level with the dome of the U.S. Capitol. From way up there you could see the fireworks at the Washington Monument on the Fourth of July. Your own independence was bursting forth. From way up there you could feel like the Capitol City was your city, your own frontyard. It was. You owned it all.

But when you finally arrived at the fourth level of the house, breathing heavily from running up the steps from the basement of the house, you feared, as you propped the heavy steel door on a tiny hook behind a wall, that the door holder would break and that you would be trapped in this god-forsaken dungeon. The rafters were enormously thick and dark. The place had the musty smell of a hundred years of clutter. The incense from the chapel would sometimes rise and mix with the appalling stench. You were in the attic!

Molly Amato, Barbara Jetter and Mary Elizabeth Lyons felt like they were punished more than anyone and were frequently sent to sit on the attic steps. Sitting there was not the problem. This punishment could be fun, just plopped down on the rickety steps, chatting away, with nothing else to do.

It was always freezing in the winter. You begged not to go to the attic during the cold months. But it was different in the summertime, when the hot air and humidity rose upward with a vengeance, like a decade of the rosary being prayed by a whole church full of devout people. You would sit by the door to the attic, placing your hands under the door hoping to feel the cool air slipping out. This kind of air conditioning worked until about April. By August it felt like the "dog days of summer" and the smell of those same dogs were locked in a cage in our attic!

If you had legitimate business up there, Sister gave you the key to open the great attic door. As you fumbled with the key you forced yourself to think about cooling down, "mind over matter" psychology, escaping from the rest of the house, because you knew it would be hotter than hell in the attic. The entire house had no air-conditioning except in the rooms the Sisters inhabited.

Click, you were in. And the adventure began. The attic went the entire length of the building, forming the letter "E." If you had specific items you had to salvage for Sister, you probably brought a laundry cart which you struggled to carry up the steps. One girl riding inside and the other girl pushing the cart and racing down a hallway on the other floors of the building was something you did when Sister was not around—no big deal. She might not even know you had done this.

But when you raced the cart in the attic it could be heard on the third floor, like thunder going from one end of the building to other. So you were careful. You needed to know the Sisters' schedule for vespers and meals. Timing was extremely important. Don't make Sister come all the way up there to remind you that, "You were not raised in a barn, young lady!"

The Halloween parties in the attic were memorable. To choose a costume to wear for the annual Halloween party, you were allowed to go through huge wooden trunks, old enough to have been donated by Abraham Lincoln himself. And dusty. You could have just put a box of costumes away one week, then come back to the attic to find them covered in several inches of dust the next week. The trunks were located throughout the attic, scattered by groups, forcing you to visit the darker and more macabre-looking areas of the top floor.

You were scared silly but there was something alluring about this area of the attic. It reeked of a different odor, almost exotic. Trunk after trunk of costumes, a Hollywood wardrobe room probably did not have as many choices. If you chose to have an Irish costume, you were in luck. Sister Mary Frances almost never reused the costumes from year to year for her annual St. Patrick's Day Show, so there were hundreds of outfits to choose from.

But, not to be limited to a show business wardrobe, there was an ample supply of grotesque animal or hideous, ghostly-goblin-monster outfits from which to choose. A bit musty, but spectacular, there was not a single one of those cheap costumes, boxed in that gaudy orange with the plastic insert to display the costume choice, so popular at People's Drug Store or G.C. Murphy's.

These costumes in boxes had a tacky plastic mask that would cut your face if you were not careful. The masks in our attic were made of a supple rubber that resembled gruesome human or animal flesh. Bela Legosi and Vincent Price would have felt right at home in this attic.

Amidst the bats, real, and the pigeons, also real, the older girls provided a celebration that would make ghosts in our attic shiver from fright. There was the eerie clanking of chains that came from the elevator mechanism. Very convenient for scaring the wits out of each other.

There were items to touch and to be fooled by in the dark, like grapes for eyeballs, spaghetti for intestines and a rubber glove filled with cold sand to shake hands with, which felt very corpse-like.

Mary Elizabeth Lyons did such a wonderful job of scaring everyone. She was even asked to come back after she graduated to re-create the Halloween attic scene.

Besides being the receptacle for the costumes, and the site of the events that occurred during the Halloween parties, the attic was quite functional as an attic. It did not accumulate a large volume of the usual clutter that most old homes with an attic tend to collect. Considering that there were up to 150 residents in this home, it was relatively clutter free. But it had its share of broken lamps, tables and fans, and boxes of clothing, sitting, waiting for further orders to serve their next owners.

When we were in high school, Julie Camden was fascinated with the story of the Holocaust. She read *Diary of Anne Frank* and at least a dozen other books on the persecution of the Jewish people. We imagined that Anne Frank's environment, when she was in hiding, might have looked very much like our attic at St. Vincent's. We sat wistfully for hours, staring out of the windows of the attic, reflecting on Anne Frank's tale of "imprisonment."

You couldn't see the Potomac River from the attic but there were plenty of government landmarks that reminded you that the city was "beneath" you literally, and in our vivid imaginations, figuratively as well.

For Julie and me, the ability to go to the attic and sit alone with our thoughts, safe in our home, was what we considered freedom. We felt privileged.

Filling Up and Filling Out

Food! Glorious food. Growing girls, we could never get enough to eat. Maybe they gave us enough. It just seemed we could never fill our starving little bodies. We had three square meals a day and sometimes a snack in the evening. Everyone looked healthy and no one ever suffered from malnutrition. Still, it was never enough.

A typical breakfast was a bowl of cereal with sliced bananas and milk, or an egg, scrambled or hardboiled, and a slice of toast. We looked forward to the days when a slice of scrapple, maybe two pieces if you lined up at the cart twice, or a lonely little link sausage was served. But six out of seven days a week, we had our old standby, which we mocked at every opportunity.

"Ladies and gentlemen, today in the dining room we are featuring, in this sturdy little plastic institutional bowl, a delicious, vitamin filled, made of grain straight from the heartland, not popped from guns, not shot from cannons, no snap*crackle*pop, just chewless pleasure that tickles the palate, guaranteed to fill you, to thrill you, to unchill you, to zap the bad oils from your inners, to make your hair and outers shine, and to pump in nutrients to nourish winners, from the Quaker man on the box with the smiling face and rosy cheeks, won't need anything else for weeks and weeks, hot, steaming, hearty, down–the–hatch OATMEAL!"

If we were home for lunch, you had a bowl of soup or a sandwich, never both, and a dish of fruit. On school days we packed a lunch, something we hated doing for two reasons: our lunches were never as good as other kids at school, and we just hated packing lunch. A sandwich made with a single slice of baloney just couldn't compete with having some leftover meatloaf, or a big roasted turkey leg from a Thanksgiving meal that no one in the family could stuff inside himself.

There were crummier lunches still—a cheese sandwich with mayonnaise or salami with mustard. Some call it bologna. To us it was just plain baloney! The worst sandwich fixin' had to be liverwurst, sliced thick and not too appetizing, with the band of plastic still around the edges. It didn't matter whether you remembered to take this plastic off or not, because you were going to throw the whole sandwich out before you got to school anyway.

No meat was to be eaten on Friday. That was the Church's rule. For our Friday, no-meat lunches, there might be a bowl of tuna or egg salad, already mixed with mayonnaise, that you would have to fight over to get your share. The bowls were always skimpy. Sometimes, in order to avoid embarrassment from someone at school seeing your puny little sandwich, you just skipped making a sandwich that day.

You always had a piece of fruit and a pack of cookies, or a Hostess cupcake with the dark chocolate frosting and the white icing swiggles on top. These little snacks always looked tasty in the packages at the DGS or a grocery store when you were ogling the goodies and had no money. But for some reason, when you brought a pack to school, they paled by comparison to someone's homemade brownies or chocolate chip cookies.

Oranges were my favorite fruit but they could be kind of messy to eat in such a short lunch period and without cutting it ahead of time. An African-American girl in my class showed me how to eat an orange without peeling it. She was proud to use the "N" word to tell me her secret:

"You nigger-lip cigarettes and you nigger-lip an orange too. Just bite off a little circle of the skin about an inch around, put it up to your lips and just suck it till you get all of the juice. Keep squeezing it real hard. The stringy stuff will go in your mouth too."

Ingenious! It sure was neater than peeling the whole thing and having the juice go everywhere. This way you got every little piece of juice and pulp in your mouth!

The little girls carried a tin lunch box sporting Roy Rogers and Dale Evans or the Mouseketeers on the sides. When you graduated into paper bags to carry your prized lunch to school, you only received two bags a week, one on Mondays, another on Wednesdays, and had to fold it up and carry it home for the next day. This was a major source of embarrassment at school in front of the other children.

By dinnertime, always five o'clock, you were famished. We had the same meals on the same days. Roast beef, mashed potatoes with gravy, lima beans on Mondays. There was always spaghetti with meatballs on Wednesdays. Fish, boiled potatoes, and stewed tomatoes on Fridays. In between days there could be beef stew made from Monday's leftover beef, hamburger patties, meatloaf— anything that you could top with thick brown gravy. Fried chicken, chopped chicken, boiled or broiled chicken, with a potato, and canned fruits and vegetables from *Nifda* or *Sexton*, or other great institutional wholesalers in the area.

There were trucks from the Claxton Food Company that came and went from St. Vincent's. Supposedly, they carried seafood products. But we never had real shrimp or crabs—the kind of seafood we used to get at the Wharf in Southwest when we were home with Dad. I must admit to being "a FISHionado!" Anything that swims or floats in water is appealing to me. And the blue crabs from the Carolinas were the pride of the wharf, costing about $1.00 a dozen in the 1950s to considerably more in the new millennium. The only seafood we saw at St. Vincent's was breaded fish sticks or patties for Friday night dinner. No butterfish fried to crispy perfection. No jumbo shrimp, steamed and flavored. It was not very appetizing but it filled you up.

It was about as wholesome as any other institutional food item in a tin can could be, but it was not what we considered to be "homemade meals." They were just "simply made meals." Desserts were Jell-O, fruit or cake. I can't ever remember having a fresh tossed green salad.

Although our biggest complaint was that there simply was not enough to eat, we had to finish everything on our plates. There were no exceptions. That meant that the white corn hominy, something only fit for pigs on a farm, and the curdliest cottage cheese in the U.S. was going to go down your throat or else.

MM and I each had our share of "or else," which meant hours and hours of staring at something on your plate that you detested, long after everyone else had finished dinner, done their homework, and then gotten ready for bed. All of the attempts to make you feel guilty about not eating a beautifully prepared meal did not work. It didn't matter that you could not watch TV till you finished your dinner. The taste and texture of some food was intolerable. It mattered very little that the poor children in Bolivia did not have such fine meals. You would gladly have shared with them on many occasions!

MM, with her great gag reflex, hated cauliflower and vomited it up after being forced to eat it. Sister then threatened her with having to eat that. Fortunately, hominy, cottage cheese and cauliflower were not served on the same day, so I was not at the "after dinner" party with her. I don't know if she really went through with her "second helping" of cauliflower.

Occasionally we got spaghetti twice in a week, or hot dogs and beans served with lettuce and tomato. The meals on weekends were much better, but of course you might not be home for these meals. Miss Emma usually fixed grilled cheese sandwiches for Saturday lunches, quite an undertaking for up to 100 girls. Sunday afternoon's hot lunch was always creamed chicken over rice. It never competed with Dad's chicken *adobo* but I always looked forward to the Sunday meal.

For dessert we had neopolitan in the little paper wrappers that would never come off right, with the three strips of chocolate, vanilla and strawberry ice cream.

Condiments like ketchup, mustard and mayonnaise were critical to making the simply-prepared food more palatable. Everyone has her own story of "stealing" food from the kitchen. Sometimes you might even volunteer to help in the kitchen in case there were leftovers the cooks would give you.

Aunt Edna bought us a Pillsbury baking oven one year for Christmas. It came complete with a light bulb to provide the heat inside the little stove, all of the pots, pans and utensils and little boxes of cake mix and biscuits for mixing and baking. We would beg Dad to buy us refills of the cake mixes in the toy store. He tried to convince us to buy Jiffy pie and cake mixes but we insisted that only Pillsbury kits would work in our oven. They were delicious!

MM and I would brag about the kind of food we got when we went home with our family. Our Dad was an excellent cook who could make even plain sea shell macaroni taste like a gourmet meal. He worked for a retired Army officer and prepared three square meals a day for him. They had to be well planned, and served only on the finest china his closet could hold. His boss bought him a new cooking range in the 1950s that sported a large grill in the center. So the kitchen at 2359 Ashmead Place, Northwest, in addition to hosting feasts with simple ingredients, also contained what we considered to be exotic—artichokes, hearts of palm, fresh lump crabmeat, filet mignon, and the like.

The St. Vincent candy shoppe supplemented our meals. In the summertime, Sister always gave us a chance to buy candy bars from the candy shoppe. It was a locked abandoned room in the basement, complete with two huge glass candy counters loaded down with at least 50 varieties of penny candy and 5¢ candy bars. BB Bats, Mary Jane's, Sugar Babies, Hershey Bars, both kinds, Skybars—you name it, the candy shoppe had it!

It may not have been as scrumptious as a couple of pieces of Velati's caramels, but it far surpassed the candy counters at the Newton or Village Theatres and the prices were much more reasonable. Sister would also open the candy shoppe before our Friday evening movies in the auditorium.

Every afternoon, someone from each group would go to the main kitchen in the basement and give the cooks a headcount for dinner. Then at five o'clock it was time to pick up the *cart* from the kitchen. The cart was made of steel, had several shelves with a ledge around the sides to avoid spillage. It rolled on wheels and was fairly easy to maneuver when it was empty. Miss Emma or Miss Betty would load it down with the large institutional serving trays with lids and wish you luck as you made it up the elevator to Sister and the dinner-waiting girls in your group, pushing and pulling, fearing an accident that would upset your cart.

On your way to the kitchen, down the back steps, you had to pass a life-size statue of St. Joseph, whose penetrating green eyes scared any second grader in Group One. The statue was on the first floor landing near the stairs that led to the basement. Many intimidating thoughts would fill the mind of a bashful seven-year-old on her trip to visit Miss Emma in the main kitchen.

"I gotta climb the back stairs. I feel like a scaredy cat. Sister said to tell Miss Betty we only have six girls for dinner."

"Six girls for dinner?" I told Sister, "I'm so hungry, I could eat all six of 'em all by myself."

"Young lady, you are impudent!"

"I'm such a big girl, I can go to the kitchen all by myself. From Group One on the third floor all the way down to the kitchen in the basement—it's about a hundred miles away. I gotta pass St. Joseph on the first floor but I can't look at his eyes, he looks like he's alive! I should ask St. Bernadette. The Blessed Mother appeared to her when she was a little girl. And I bet she wasn't a scaredy cat."

"O, you're Miss Emma. You're not Miss Betty. Just six, Miss Emma."

"Six what? Ain't gone help you be bashful and don't speak up. Girl, you got some chunky cheeks on you. What group you in"

"First, but Sister's moving me to second when school's out. Wow, is that statue the Kitchen Madonna? It's pretty."

"Don't stall. Go on back up the steps, lil girl!"

"I am. I am. How can I forget about it, gotta pass St. Joseph again. I am, you are, she is, he is, he is ALIVE! No, please St. Joseph, don't come to life. O Lord, I am not worthy. O St. Joseph, I am not worthy. Don't look at his eyes. Good, second floor, now don't look back. Phew, safe, third floor. I'm back!"

When Catherine DeForge was a teenager she helped make "butter" in the kitchen. She would put food coloring in a vat of lard to turn it yellow. She swore she'd never eat margarine when she grew up.

After dinner, the girl in each group who had "cart duty" would bring the cart back to the main kitchen and wash the pots and pans in the huge hopper, already filled with bubbling soapy water. This soap was especially hard on your hands. It was homemade LYE soap!

There was quite an extensive process involved in the making of this soap. Miss Emma would pour the liquid lye mixture into deep, large industrial-size cake pans, let it cool for a hour, then cut the mixture when it hardened into large bars of soap.

The bars, about 20 of them, would be tossed into a large empty tin can that Mr. Boykins had punched holes in. He made a handle out of heavy wire and inserted this into two holes at the top of the can. Voila! A bucket-type gadget that you raised and lowered in hot water to make it sudsy. You were then ready to do the pots and pans.

The counter to the sink was high; too bad if you were short. But the cooks remembered to place a stool there so that you had no excuse for not taking care of their pots and pans like a professional in a five-star restaurant.

When the lye soap shrunk down in size to small one or two-inch cubes, it resembled Velati's caramels, Washington's most famous and best tasting candy. Velati's was a candy shop at 9th and F Streets, Northwest. It was in an old building with tall glass windows that let in the light, and let the customers view the caramel-making process from the street. You saw everything, from the pouring of the hot liquid into large pans, to the finish, with the clerks beating away at the huge mounds of candy with little metal hammers. There were hard-chewy and soft-crumbly caramels, some with and some without nuts, and chocolate and vanilla flavored candies to choose from.

Having cart duty at St. Vincent's and having to use the lye soap felt like punishment. Receiving Velati's caramels was always like a reward. Ironic how the process for making lye soap and Velati's caramels was so similar!

There were no hard and fast etiquette-of-eating rules in the dining room. There was no Emily Post as a guide. You just ate and Sister would correct your manners and your mannerisms as you went along. We were probably very young when we learned to cut our own meat with a knife. I am grateful that along the way someone enforced the custom of holding the fork in your left hand, tongs turned down, knife in the right hand, both utensils in a somewhat horizontal position. It seems more Europeans eat this way. The first time I saw a man hold his fork vertically in his fist with the other hand "sawing" away at the meat I was at the Hot Shoppes on Connecticut Avenue. I wanted to reprimand him for what I considered a display of poor table manners. How uncivilized. Sister would not have approved of his table manners.

There were several Hot Shoppes Restaurants around the City. We ate there with volunteers or family whenever we got the chance or had the money. If we were downtown shopping many times we pooled our money together to go to Eddie Leonard's Sandwich Shop. It was amazing how many times you could cut a portion off from a footlong submarine to satisfy an orphan girl's hunger.

Jamie and I got locked in the walk-in refrigerator. It was a Friday evening and we both had been to our respective schools' games. We proceeded to look for something to eat other than the usual fried eggs and stewed tomatoes, the standard Friday evening meal that Sister Bernard had saved us in little aluminum plates. It was never very tasty after being warmed for three hours in the oven.

So we went to the main kitchen. With wide open doors and no cooks around, we investigated the grub in the 8'x 8'x 8' walk-in refrigerator in the back of the main kitchen. Crates of raw eggs. Heads of cabbage. Bags of apples. Huge plastic vats of potato salad. Gallon-size condiment jars of mayonnaise, mustard and catsup. All this food and not a piece of bread nor a spoon in sight!

We started back toward the door to find other goodies that might be more accessible and realized the door had locked behind us. It felt colder the longer we were in there but we did not panic. We felt sure the cooks would re-check all of the doors before they locked up for the evening.

Fortunately, several girls in our group noticed we were missing. They told us later that when they found us missing they immediately came downstairs to the kitchen to look for us. I guess we had a reputation for feeding our faces. Where else would we have been? It was a chilling experience for both of us.

It was always a treat to eat out. Most of our eating out, though, was not in restaurants, but outdoors in the Grove. If the humidity were low on some summer evenings, Sister might have the girl with cart duty wheel the cart down the cement pathway to a picnic table outside.

On the Feast of St. Vincent, the 19th of July, we had special box lunches outside. The cooks worked for hours to produce 100 or so crunchy fried chicken dinners, complete with dinner rolls, coleslaw and applesauce.

Even a humble meal felt like a celebration when we ate in the Grove. On several occasions in the winter Sister Alma took us outside for a real weenie roast. Everyone roasted their own hot dogs and marshmallows on sticks scavenged from the bounty of leafless trees in the Grove.

Eating out was carried to extremes in Sister Bernard's high school group. On weekends there were usually fewer than 10 girls home for meals. She often let us go to McDonald's for dinner. This was no easy feat! McDonald's was on South Dakota Avenue, only about three miles away, so we had to take a bus to get there. We had no cars, nor anyone to drive us there.

The day it was my turn to pick up the food, I went with Jamie and Terri Conner. We walked to College Pharmacy to catch the bus that took us a few blocks beyond Providence Hospital. Then we transferred buses to go out South Dakota Avenue. If you arrived at the first bus stop on time, it was a 35-minute trip one-way. Ordering the food took about 10 minutes—fast food service seemed to be fast in those days. Twenty cheeseburgers, twenty hamburgers, twenty-three orders of French fries—an extra for each of the food deliverers!—and twenty Coca-Colas. All items were 20 cents each, and just a few cents more for the cheeseburgers.

Back on the bus, we were careful not to spill the Cokes that they had packaged so carefully for us. The fries were hot and crunchy, and well worth making the trip to get everyone else's food. No one on the bus seemed to mind the three of us feeding our faces like little piggies. We agreed among ourselves that it was perfectly fine to take a few extra fries from each order. No one would notice and they would be cold when we got home anyway.

A little more than an hour and we returned, with burgers, fries and Cokes still in tact. Mission accomplished. Everyone was grateful for the treat. No one cared that the food was not hot—we got to eat out again!

Sister Bernard was always indulging us with food—the one vice we could explore. She always made us pots of coffee in the morning. And somehow she always managed to find fresh rolls or pastries to go with the coffee. For several years she managed to get donations of English muffins which rounded out our breakfasts and snacks very well. She herself was very thin and seemed to enjoy watching us gorge ourselves with as many pastries or muffins as we desired.

The Cuban girls had a special way of making coffee, *café con leche*, that used a lot more milk. The Sisters were not supposed to eat or drink in front of us. Sister took a sip of the coffee once, then said with her emphatically Boston accent, "To make sure the milk was not sour." I think she was just intrigued by the Cuban coffee.

Eating at McDonald's was wonderful. But when we really wanted to have a finer meal in a more tasteful setting, several of us took it upon ourselves to go the extra mile. Literally, we went several miles—by bus—to take ourselves out to some of the best restaurants our savings could afford. For several years, the Frank sisters Terrie and Ginger, Jamie and I celebrated our birthdays together. Although our birthdays were at different times of the year—Jamie's birthday and mine happened to be in the Spring—we planned our excursions in warmer weather to avoid the harshness of the winter.

Dressed to impress any young gentlemen we might meet in our travels, one year we took the bus to a French restaurant in Georgetown. Another year we took a bus, with a bus transfer or two, and a taxicab ride to dine at Hall's on the River, a wonderful seafood restaurant just a few miles from the Wharf at Maine Avenue, Southwest.

There was a great restaurant in the country which we went to when we could get a ride—the Peter Pan Inn. It was all the way in Urbana, Maryland, quite a long hike from D.C. and no public transportation to get us there. Of course, Paris, Madrid and Milano were not on our travel itineraries, but there was no reason not to enjoy a little bit of the culture for an evening meal from time to time. After all, money can buy you anything and no one had to know that you lived in an orphanage.

Crinolines to Pillbox Hats

There were no Barbie dolls around St. Vincent's. In fact, there were very few dolls around at all. The ones we did have were more like realistic, cuddly infants, without male or female features and anatomical parts. No one cared about being "politically correct" in those days.

Almost everyone collected *Ginny* dolls. Each doll about eight inches tall, they featured international outfits. They were not too expensive and they did not disappear off the shelves before you were able to collect a few from the series. You could also buy little foot lockers that looked like miniature steamer trunks to store their wardrobes. These, along with another great invention for little girls— paper dolls—kept us busy for hours, changing doll clothes, designing doll clothes and kindling a fascination with real fashions for ourselves.

We were fashion plates—just could not have enough clothing, always had to be shopping for clothing. We loved showing off our new duds and dreamed of having nicer clothing than the next girl— from a tender age of about eight years old.

Consequently, to have your initials written on your clothing was a most discomforting event. Sister would actually take a marker with indelible, permanent ink to identify each piece of your clothing. Inevitably, a very conspicuous location was chosen to print your initials. However innocently executed, these labels, bleeding through the cloth to expose your secret, just shouted out *"Look at me—I'm an orphan!"* Now the whole world knew.

Every time you unthinkingly took off your shoes in public, there was your telltale set of initials—*JM*—on the bottom of your foot. If you forgot to pull your undershirt down into your belt, and it showed outside the collar of your blouse, there it was again, your billboard advertising your misfortune to be living in an orphanage.

At home, your washcloth and towel were also marked with your initials. This was irritating, but a lot less stigmatizing than presenting your initials in this way at school. Fortunately, it had very little impact on your social life. Your washcloth and towel were kept in the bathroom on your own little two-pronged hook. They were hung alphabetically.

If you did not feel like taking a bath one night, you had to remember to soak down the washcloth and towel, and dampen your hair on the ends, as though you had taken care of your daily hygiene. It was one less day a week that you had to battle the lye soap, or worse yet, the annoying floating Ivory soap that dried your skin out as much as the lye soap.

MM and I used to bring a bottle of Prell from home so we wouldn't have to use the usual drying shampoo. Sister must have gotten a donation from a generous donor and for a period of about six months we had a thick, green-colored, luxurious shampoo to wash our hair. She said it was Hawaiian shampoo. It smelled sweet and you didn't mind the usual drudgery of leaning over the hopper in the bathroom to wash your hair every few days. After you wrapped your towel around your hair in turban fashion, you felt like you had just been to a spa.

I don't know what the Sisters were so worried about, we dressed and behaved very "modestly"—both in the sense that we did not spend a lot for clothing and also that our clothing was in good taste, not too revealing.

It may have been different with other generations of girls, but during my days at St. Vincent's, from age six to almost eighteen, we could have won prizes for live modesty demonstrations. No one saw anyone totally in the buff!

From the time you wore cotton undershirts in Group One, which were chosen to cover your little "mosquito bites" on your chest, you looked for ways to remove your underwear without showing a trace of skin. It was the dance of modesty. A blouse with buttons down the front was removed with as little attention drawn to one's self as possible.

Standing facing your locker, you would throw your nightgown over your head, then nimbly remove your undershirt and slip your arms in the nightgown. With your nightgown pulled down over your body, waddling around like Chilly Willy, the penguin, your skirt was easy to remove and nothing showed.

In the bathhouse, a wet bathing suit presented a challenge but somehow, using the same prim-and-proper techniques as your clothing and underwear, you were able to dress and undress without being exposed to the world.

In the older groups and in high school, one could simply slip behind a bathroom stall to change clothes. There were a few girls who paraded around in their underwear or purposely danced around, humming the stripper song, as they undressed. But we were, on the whole, very modest. The goal was reached and revelations were minimal—no cracks were spotted, no cleavage displayed!

The rage in the 1950s and early 1960s was the crinoline. It was no ordinary half-slip. It was the mesh skeleton you wore under your skirt or dress to give it "poof." To give your crinoline that puffy quality that resembled Anna's clothing from *The King and I*, you had to soak your crinoline in sugar water, then hang it out to dry. The best place for drying your crinoline was the porch, where you could leave it in a circle to dry and stiffen to perfection.

When you wore it, you had to remember to sit or stand properly, holding the crinoline down when you sank in a chair. Of course it was literally impossible to bend over wearing a crinoline and remain modest. But it was very stylish to have just a teeny bit of the mesh net fabric trail a quarter of an inch below your skirt. That was about as seductive and risque as we knew how to be at age 10.

In high school, "petti-pants" were popular. They were like a half-slip but not open, they had legs and were like a pair of panties that went to just above your knees. The frillier and lacier they were the better. For something so new on the market, they were unusually cheap and Lerner's downtown had the best selection. We used them under our cheerleading uniforms at St. Patrick's. Sister did not complain when we hiked up our outfits because as we twirled and did handstands and jumps, we showed off silk and lace rather than panties and bare skin.

Someone in the community donated fabric to our group one year. It was a generous gift and Sister Maria accepted it graciously and made all of us beautiful full skirts with thick waste bands, a style that was very popular at the time. She even had us pose outside in the Grove and sent the photographs to the woman who donated the fabric.

The style of blouse that Amelia Peña wore with her new skirt seemed to emphasize her breasts and make it more apparent that she was long overdue for buying a bra. We had been envious because Amelia was developing a lot faster than the rest of us. So we attacked her verbally, telling her that her breasts would sag if she didn't wear a bra soon. She was embarrassed, of course. But not because we had confronted her with our newly acquired facts of life, but because she would have to ask her father to buy her a bra. The next time she went home for a weekend, she returned as a new, respectable, uplifted woman, and we left her alone.

In the 1950s, having a very little waistline was the "in" thing. We marveled at Mitzi Gaynor's teeny little 17-inch middle when we saw her perform the wonderful dance scenes in *Hit the Deck* and *White Christmas*. We would walk around holding our stomachs in a few minutes before taking our measurements to see if our statistics improved. Unfortunately, most of us hovered anywhere from a 22-inch to a 25-inch waistline. We felt like we were failures as voluptuous "pin up girls." And at 12 years old, life seemed to be over since you only had a 30 to 32 inch bustline. All of the special exercises (all ladies know these exercises!) to increase your bustline had no effect. We just had to wait till Mother Nature's "endowment" blessings kicked in when we were teenagers.

An old letter from St. Vincent's archival files turned up an interesting opinion about wearing uniforms. It was written in the early 1900s by Sister Rosalia, who was the first Superior at the new St. Vincent's on Edgewood Street.

"I do not think there would be any economy in having the children uniformed. The price of material will be the same if you buy ten pieces alike or have them assorted."

MM and I felt this was a very liberal philosophy for a Sister at the turn of the century, and agreed that uniforms, which we hated, were not necessary and not necessarily cheaper. But we found the information from Sister Rosalia's letter to be quite dated and offensive when we read the next sentence.

"The modern view of men in charge of institutions is that the institution itself marks the *inmates* sufficiently without resorting to uniform."

Inmates? Language changes so drastically. This was also the era when St. Vincent's was called *St. Vincent's Orphan Asylum.*

The girls who were placed at St. Vincent's through D.C. Public Welfare had an actual allowance for their clothing. Sister bought everything they needed—dresses, skirts, blouses, shoes and underwear. There seemed to have had an abundance of clothing, which they never outgrew because more money came every several months and they got more clothing in the next size.

Those on D.C. Public Welfare were in a minority. Almost everyone was placed at St. Vincent's through Catholic Charities. For each individual placed through Catholic Charities, the financial arrangement made with your parents for your room and board was different. I suspect that the notion of an equitable sliding fee scale did not exist in those days, because there were some parents who paid dearly and others who could not be found to pay anything once their daughter was placed.

For those of us whose parents gave us a wee bit of spending money or helped furnish us with some basic needs when we visited, Sister ran a little dress shop. She would buy good quality dresses on sale in various sizes then "sell" them to us at cost. It appeared to be a win-win situation for all. Sister selected the styles we chose, our parents did not have to shop, and we got to choose what we liked. Sound good?

Well, we didn't fall for it. We just knew Sister's motives. She wanted to control how "modest" or how revealing our dresses were. Buying the dresses assured her we would not have extra money for the goodies and junk we really wanted to buy with our money. Our parents still had to pay for the clothing. And choices—what choices did we really have.

So your wardrobe over the years was created through a combination of buying dresses when you had some money, your own worn-out uniforms, or hand-me-downs and hand-me-overs from other girls in your group. Shorts were allowed on certain occasions when you were in the younger groups. Pedal pushers could be used for some of the summer outings, if they were approved by Sister. She would try very hard to get MM and I "twin" dresses, or at least dresses with the same matching pattern with different colors.

Now in high school we had a lot more latitude. Rita McAuliff, who once lived at St. Rose's and then volunteered at St. Vincent's, took Sister Bernard and other Sisters shopping for most of our clothes. She used Bill Marean's station wagon. Occasionally, Sister gave us money for Easter and Christmas clothes and she encouraged us to shop for ourselves in downtown dress shops. Fortunately, since I went to school at St. Patrick's at 9th and G Streets, I went window shopping often. I browsed the racks for hours at Woodies, Hecht's, Lansburgh's, Kann's, Jelleff's and Garfinkel's. Morton's was the cheapest store in town and had a lot of junk. Ocassionally you could find something well made. Lerner's was much closer to the budget we had to follow, so that's where most of us shopped.

Lerner's also had a great selection of trendy Bermuda shorts, culottes, pedal pushers and capris and other sports clothing, items we were permitted to wear for summer outings only.

Your shoes could make or break your outfit. The budget usually allowed you to buy shoes from Thom McAn's or one of the other stores on F Street that displayed the white fabric shoes you could have dyed to match your dress. You never bought shoes from a department store because the prices were "out of sight." But when money was no object, Hahn's Shoe Store was the place to buy the best leather shoes. Although pointed toed "spikes"—three and four-inch heels—were popular when we were in high school, Hahn's also carried a good selection of "Cuban heels" with shorter, stubbier heels that were a lot more comfortable.

Pillbox hats and white gloves, thanks to Jacqueline Kennedy, were in fashion when we were in high school in the 1960s. Eyeglasses with "cat woman" white frames were popular too. We had to have all of these things to complete our Sunday outfits.

Because our total curriculum at St. Patrick's Academy was business and we were preparing for careers as secretaries and bookkeepers in the business world, the Holy Cross Sisters at school encouraged neat conservative, business attire. So those of us from St. Vincent's who attended St. Patrick's were given a double dose of "dressing for success" at a very early age.

Our uniform at St. Patrick's consisted of a forest green, wool A-line skirt and blazer and white shirt with a collar. The collar was worn outside of the blazer. The blazer was trimmed in crisp white piping and had embroidered emblem on the breast pocket with the words *Crux spes unica,* which, when translated literally was "Cross Hope Universal."

Saddle oxfords with white bobbie sox completed the uniform. A new style of saddle oxfords came out that had a black and a grey patch instead of a black stripe on the sides of the shoes. These were not as "sturdy" and did not last as long, but they were certainly a lot more "cool" than the traditional clod-hopper style shoes. Is it any wonder that Catholic school girls in the 1950s and 1960s looked forward to the designated "mission" days when you could donate 25 cents to simply wear "street" clothes.

The Homeplace

The first time I saw the 1970s movie version of Little Orphan Annie I felt as though I had gone back in time to my St. Vincent's days. Despite the fact that the movie depicted the 1930s era, it was an accurate reflection of my experience at St. Vincent's in the 1950s and 1960s. The clothing was just as frumpy and orphanish in style. Watching the scene with the little girls scrubbing floors and the background of beds with iron bars—it was exactly like spying through a looking glass at St. Vincent's Group Two dormitory!

Although it was a typical early 1900s red-brick style structure with the expected architectural trimmings found in such a large building, St. Vincent's layout was quite unique. It had a main building with two wings. An aerial view showed the "E" shape of the building, and a landscaped island in front of the house circled by a driveway that climbed the steep hill from Edgewood Street.

In the bottom half of the "E" was a huge concrete courtyard, entered into by way of a concrete hill leading to the back driveway where commercial vehicles made deliveries. Overlooking the courtyard, on each floor, was a huge wooden planking porch about 10 feet wide that served as an extra room without windows. Many a girl climbed over the first floor porch railing and jumped the height of one floor onto the concrete courtyard, burning her feet from the blow but thanking God for her deliverance from death.

Inside, there were great slate steps to scrub on your hands and knees and at least a dozen chandeliers hanging throughout the inside of the house for the very bold to swing on when Sister wasn't looking.

There was a set of steps, technically to be used as a fire escape, that went from the third floor to the courtyard. Running down these steps was forbidden but I never saw a girl walk unless Sister was nearby. An iron gate at the final landing of the steps could only be opened by slipping a skinny wrist through a secret opening, which you learned the first week you lived at St. Vincent's.

Inside the five-story structure was a secret stairwell that led from the massive institutional kitchen in the basement to behind the auditorium on the first floor. Then up to the secret area behind the chapel on the second floor—a great place to play "I'm the bishop—kiss my ring!" to try on the priest's vestments or use them as a cape while pretending to be a matador fighting a bull, or take a swig from the wine used for Mass, always stored away securely. The prize was finding the golden chalice.

The stairwell then made its way up to the third floor, where there was a huge pigeon-infested dormitory with painted white iron beds along the walls, usually used for visiting sisters. This sun-filled room was sometimes used as an infirmary for the girls. This wing was called "Paradise."

Since the top floor was Paradise, the bottom floor, naturally could have been referred to as "Hell" or something that resembled it, because this is where we "cut up" the most. It was the "Rumpus Room," a huge tiled playroom on the far right of the building, used by everyone at St. Vincent's regardless of age or grade in school. It was definitely the noisiest room, being strategically placed away from the Chapel and the Sister's quarters on the second floor, and it came in handy when we had flash storms in the summer for anyone playing outside to seek shelter, serving as a "holding tank" when we had outings while we waited for the bus.

The broken keys of the piano, its out-of-tune condition and the piano stool that would scratch your legs when you sat down did little to discourage the enthusiasm we expressed as we sat for hours playing "Heart and Soul" and "Chopsticks." With the exception of Amelia Peña, who had just started out, no one had taken piano lessons and no one wanted them because you might be called upon to play the organ in the chapel.

Years prior to my era at St. Vincent's, there was a gentleman, Sgt. Bodner, U.S.M.C. who directed the "St. Vincent's mini-orchestra," which consisted of girls he had taught to play violin, piano or other instruments.

Anna Neidringhaus was photographed in the assigned uniform, holding a violin which she could not play. He told her to "pretend; move the bow back and forth, but do not touch the strings!" He tried her on the drums with no success. Anna ended up on the chimes. Perhaps no true musical talent was found among the girls, and the lessons were discontinued.

The Rumpus Room was the one place where you could get away with acting like "a wild Indian," something Sister warned you against. Rollerskating indoors, usually prohibited, was more exciting in the Rumpus Room because the floors were so slick. It always seemed to be home for a couple of neighborhood dogs or cats, or a bird with a broken wing. Or maybe you wanted to play indoor croquet, or when that got tiring, dueling with the wooden mallets like Robin Hood with a sword.

Inevitably there would be a girl sitting in a big easy chair, engrossed in a book, oblivious to the noise and chaos all around her, escaping her surroundings through the written word.

School was provided at St. Vincent's in the very early days of its history, with grades one through eight, with special emphasis on sewing and embroidery, although all the traditional school subjects were taught as well. This continued through the time that St. Rose's Technical Institute closed down and moved its operation to Edgewood Street and academics centered on a high school age population.

In the late 1940s, after the school operations were finally abandoned at St. Vincent's, a major rehabilitation project was underway. The Sisters had long proposed breaking down the old congregate building into five complete units, each to be a distinct entity, much like apartments. The Director of Catholic Charities at this time was the Most Reverend Lawrence J. Shehan, who also served as the President of the Board of Trustees of St. Vincent's. The Board approved the Sisters' proposal for the rehab and while the high school girls were away at a summer camp in Maryland, the work began.

Under the new plan the groups were reorganized with Group I, caring for 6 to 8 year olds, with a capacity of 20 girls. Group II, 8 to 10 years, capacity, 19. Group III, 10 to 12 years, capacity, 17. Group IV, 12 to14 years, capacity 20. The High School Group had girls from age 14 to18 and had a capacity of 26 girls. The age range was arbitrary; mental age and physical size were also considered when placing girls in the groups.

Each group had its own living room, dining room, kitchenette, sleeping quarters, lavatories and storage space. The Groups III, IV and the high school groups had a study room. The high-school group also had a laundry.

The only sections of the house that were used in common were the chapel, the auditorium and the Rumpus Room. The cooking was done in the central kitchen and the food was taken to each group dining room on specially made service carts.

There were other rooms available for central supplies, a guests' dining room, rooms with adjoining baths for infirmaries, social workers' office and adjoining storerooms for recreation equipment and administration offices. The building was massive.

Orphan, Heal Thyself!

My daughter, Kristina Heidler Conner, is a doctor of naturopathic medicine. She was born a decade after I left St. Vincent's but she assures me that the medical care given to us at St. Vincent's is the same professional care she would have recommended for us. The truth is, we had NO medical care. That is, we never saw a doctor on a regular basis!

Doctors of naturopathic medicine have seven principles they follow that guide them, many of which were compatible with the philosophy of the administration of St. Vincent's, such as these: The "Healing power of nature"—the body has the ability to establish, maintain and restore health, and "Prevention is the best cure"—promote life habits that create good health.

When we first went to St. Vincent's we were at the end of the era when doctors made "house calls." In my Aunt's Capitol Hill neighborhood, we would go to Dr. Hodges' office to get the needed immunizations. He lived across the street from us, and he came to our house on many occasions—sometimes to give the children a shot and other times to have a drink with the uncles. All of the youngsters caught chicken pox and mumps and it was easier for him to come to us than to have Aunt Edna take a sick child to his office. The house visit most vivid in my memory is the one about a week after I had came home from the hospital from a tonsillectomy. He teasingly reminded me that I should only have popsicles that soon after my tonsils were removed, and that perhaps I should have not swallowed a dime until *after* my throat was healed.

Certainly there was a physician on retainer for St. Vincent's. But to my knowledge, in my twelve years of affiliation with St. Vincent's, no one visited a doctor on a regular basis. The services of the Emergency Room at Providence Hospital were nearby for true emergencies. Providentially, we were healthy. We had a stable, consistent routine of sleeping at least eight hours a night, we ate well, we were involved in lots of exercise, and without exception, we went outside in the sunshine every day.

Perhaps all of those things they tell you about being sociable and being in the company of other people is true—it wards off depression. We were, most often, very happy.

There is a seam from a cut on my hand, which occurred when I was about eight years old. I jumped off the swing when I heard the Angelus bell, which rang every day at noon and at six o'clock p.m. The cut was deep enough to have required stitches but I do not remember having them or even being checked by a doctor.

With the amount of candy and sweets we ate, and the lack of fluoride in the water, it's a wonder more of the girls did not have bad teeth. MM and I seemed to be the only ones that went to a dentist. Dad took us to the low-cost dental clinic at Providence Hospital when he could get an appointment on his one day off a week. He paid on a sliding-fee scale so it was somewhat affordable. Later we went to Georgetown University's dental clinic which was even more affordable.

There were two occasions that did require the services of an emergency room doctor. When Jamie was in the eighth grade, she got a splinter in her leg from playing on the wood and iron merry-go-round in the Grove. It became so infected she was unable to walk and was finally taken to the ER at Providence Hospital. They told her she could have lost her leg and that she was lucky. The worst that happened to her was that she had to be on crutches a while.

Another time I accompanied Jamie to a doctor's office in Brookland, a mile from St. Vincent's. We walked there and Jamie had an EKG done. She checked out okay and we walked back home, having made her second doctor visit at the age of 15.

Watch Your Language, Young Lady!

You always had to be on guard about what you said, how you said it and most importantly, the words you chose to express it. Your words could be fatal. You could be "campused" for the slightest little infraction and you had to be knowledgeable about which words were accepted. MM and I had a favorite song that got us in trouble when we had the misfortune to sing it at the wrong time to the wrong listener:

"All the girls in France do not wear their underpants
And the dance they do is enough to kill a Jew
And the suits they wear are enough to freeze a bear
And the bear they freeze would bring a sheik down to his knees..."

Of course there was a little belly dancing and hip wiggling we did with the song.

Sister severely reprimanded us for these tasteless lyrics, especially if the entire group joined in the song and dance routine. But that only reinforced our bad behavior. We enjoyed substituting new words to show off our cleverness with words. The dirtier the better! We were very careful to switch *bears* for *girls* and the word *blank* for *Jews* if we thought Sister was close at hand.

There are a gazillion jump rope and hand-clapping songs we knew that still resound within your head: *"Blue bells, cocker shells....she sang, she sang, she sang so sweet,......how many kisses did she receive?"*

There were words Sister would use whose tone alone clued you in—you were in trouble: Young lady, Missssssss Mondoñedo, Missy, You there girl, Child! Sister never really gave commands, she never really told you what to do. She would just say, "It would BEHOOVE you to ....!"

We actually used words and phrases like *swell* and *gee whiz* and *you betcha*! Here is a glossary of some special terms and phrases used by the girls and associates at St. Vincent's.

ANGELUS—A prayer said at 6:00 a.m., 12 noon and 6:00 p.m. When you heard the bell ring, whether you were indoors or outside, you stopped everything, bowed your head and prayed.

AW, I'M TELLIN' SISTER—The tattle tails' and manipulators' greatest threat was to tell Sister the "truth" or at least her version of the truth.

BOOK—This is Sister's accounting system, how much spending money you have to spend your whole life; it's in the book!

BROOKLAND—The area around Catholic University, which included St. Anthony's Church, school and parish hall, Fred's Restaurant & Bar, the Newton Theater, Baldwin's Bake Shop and the Brookland Hardware Store.

CU—Catholic University, just a pleasant tree-lined, one-mile walk away.

CAMPUSED/GROUNDED—Punished, you screwed up, and you must pay the price.

CART/FOOD!—The food comes from the kitchen to each group on the cart. Whoever has "cart-duty," has to go to the kitchen pick it up and bring it up to the girls.

CELL—A little bedroom exclusively for each Sister. It even resembled what we imagined a jail cell would look like.

CIRCLE—To the east of the building, close to the field used for baseball. The circle was a quiet concrete walkway near the woods and mulberry, pear and apple trees. A great getaway.

COLLEGE PHARMACY—The drugstore of the same name next to Dickey's Laundry and across the street from the DGS.

COURTYARD—Concreted area in the back of the house, perfect for roller skating.

DGS—District Grocery Store. Almost every corner in Washington, D.C. had these convenience stores where you could cash in your soda bottles for pennies or buy anything from soap powder, to dill pickles from a barrel, to penny candy.

DUTY—Your job, your weekly chore. Everybody gets one, everybody hates them, but it's your duty! Some were harder than others, like bathroom cleanup vs. Venetian blinds.

FOREVER IN OUR HEARTS—Response to a quick prayer: "Live Jesus, forever in our hearts." Forever in our hearts—truly the place where our experience of living at St. Vincent's dwells.

The GATE—The gate leading out of the back of the property closest to the pool onto Edgewood Street, which was really a fence and had no gate. The gate was a landmark for meeting up with your friends who were in a different group on the way to or from school or the DGS.

GRIFFITH CONSUMERS—The oil people whose trucks parked in the concrete courtyard area and filled the tanks in the boiler room.

GROTTO—At the back edge of the property along the fence line, the grotto, a replica of the Grotto at Lourdes, included a beautiful life-size statue of our Lady of Lourdes. It was surrounded by a stone walled altar.

GROUP—Your battalion, your age group, your *jail-mate* group. St. Vincent's was divided into five groups; groups were divided by your grade in school. Each group had its own living room, dining room, dormitory, lavatory and kitchenette. In the 1960s there were only four groups, two of which were actually for high-school aged girls.

The GROVE—Outside, the great outdoors, our backyard, a large playground with a circular walkway, complete with a merry-go-round, swings, sandbox, monkey bars, sliding board and picnic tables and grotto devoted to our Lady of Lourdes.

The HILL—The front hill, a long, curved driveway leading from Edgewood Street to the front of the building, great for sleigh riding in the winter and skating and bicycling in the summer.

HOME FOR GOOD—Leaving St. Vincent's to live somewhere else, usually with your own family but possibly because of adoption or going to a foster home.

HOPPER—The oversized utility sink in the lavatory where we washed our hair and the dirty mops and emptied our dirty water buckets.

The INCINERATOR—A real honest-to-goodness iron and brick rip-roaring fire incinerator with an opening approximately 4'x4' where we emptied trash cans. Just outside of the main kitchen, site of a lot of thought-provoking stories about Hell and damnation.

KRISKAN—(excuse the spelling; never really saw this word in print, believe it to be the German word for Christ child) The person whose name you chose to buy a gift for at Christmas time.

LAVATORY—Not just the sink, but the whole bathroom. "Lavatory" was the most dreaded duty of them all.

MEA CULPA—Literally, from the Latin, *my fault*, usually said as part of a prayer. We utilized it facetiously to express the sentiment, *well, excuuuse me!* or *Yes, I AM guilty* after carrying out some forbidden action.

Your NEIGHBOR—That meant *her*, over there, *that girl*, your sister in Christ, the one sitting next to you, used when Sister did not want to name names but you knew who she meant.

ORPHAN/ORPHANAGE—Fighting words, words we hated, but words that truly described our situation and our home.

PARADISE—An infirmary for isolation for girls with a contagious illness or some bad behavioral situation going on. In the summer it was used by visiting sisters who attended Catholic University. It was the highest room in all of the house, in the middle wing, above the chapel. We thought it was located there so that you were close to heaven in the event you died from an illness.

PARLOR—A tastefully-decorated room on the first floor just across from the office and main entrance that was reserved for guests. An impressive room we stayed out of.

PRIVILEGED CHARACTER—Spoiled, "Sister's pet," or someone who broke the rules. It also referred to a girl whose parents, although not wealthy, had "class."

PLAYCLOTHES—Everyone had a Sunday outfit, complete with

pillbox hat and gloves; everything else you wore were your play clothes. We couldn't wear blue jeans or shorts. The closest thing to being normal or cool was wearing leggings in the winter with your heavy coat. We ended up with quite a collection of raggedy skirts, blouses and dresses.

REFECTORY- Where the nuns ate; their dining room.

RUMPUS ROOM—Large playroom in the basement that had a usually-broken down piano, a record player and lots of junky furniture. This was the one area where girls from all groups could mingle. It came in handy when we had flash storms in the summer; everyone playing outside would seek shelter here.

SACRISTY—The room next to the chapel where the priest puts on special *vestments* to prepare for Mass or other church services.

SANCTUARY—A safe area such as inside the house when bullies from the neighborhood were chasing you home. You sought sanctuary.

SATURDAY DUTY—The routine for weekly cleaning, especially the floors. It usually included dust mopping, wet mopping, waxing, and finally *weighting*, shining, the floors.

SCULLERY—Room where dishes are done, a kitchen with only a sink. Every group's dining room had one.

SEAS-STAIR—The word "sister" said with a Spanish accent. I thought it meant *abracadabra*, like magic, because the Cuban girls used it on Sister and got whatever they wanted. Like *"Seas-stair, I need some Sweeetheart Soap"* or *"Seas-stair, I have to go chopping (shopping) after schoool. Okay Seas-stair?"*

SHRINE—This was our version of a "wonder of the world," a work in progress, the National Shrine of the Immaculate Conception, eighth largest church in the world, one mile from our back gate to whose building fund we contributed from the time we could spell *immaculate conception*, maybe age eight years old.

SISTER SAID—This phrase was a prefacer, especially for the self-righteous, goody-goody two shoes tattletales of the group. When someone passed along Sister's messages, used especially when the announcement was something unpopular and you did not want the rest of the group to shoot the messenger.

STANLEY'S—A *five and dime store* at 4th and Rhode Island Avenue that had everything from rick-rack to metal taps to nail to your shoes.

We always shopped there for new school supplies every September.

TOKEN—No political connotation, a token was a coin used on Capitol Transit for car fare worth about a dime.

TOMBSTONE TERRITORY—An area in the woods to the side of the property where a dozen or more huge 10 ft. marble slabs had been discarded. They were perfect stages for any kind of play or show, including re-enactments of Jesus praying in the desert, cowboy and Indian shoot-'em-ups, or, most perfect of all, for playing games of "visiting the haunted graveyards."

TRINITY—Notwithstanding the real Trinity of God the Father, God the Son and God The Holy Ghost, Trinity is a girls' college less than a mile away. It was the source of so many wonderful volunteers. They were like big sisters, they were like mentors, they were like friends.

TURKEY THICKET—A park in Brookland, just beyond the Newton Theater at 12th Street.

WEIGHT—A floor buffer for shining tile floors. We had to "weight" the floors every day and wash, wax and weight them on weekends.

The WOODS—The area to the front and side of the property which abutted commercial property on Fourth Street, blessed with several weeping willow trees, brimming over with poison ivy, poison oak and poison sumac.

YALE—Not a university, but a laundry service, whose truck came twice a week to pick up our dirty laundry.

A Sister

The word *Sister* in my world deserves a capital S. It's an important word. And to have a sister is a phenomenal concept. Everyone should have a little sister. It becomes a test in defending her, outwitting her, molding and scolding her—truly a test of one's patience. More than just a test of one's patience, being a big sister is a privileged exercise in caring and sharing and growing.

Most of the time I was proud to be Maggie's big sister and I would have fought anyone who tried to hurt her or put her down. She's the one who was with me in the flesh as a child, from her birth, to our childhood days at St. Vincent's, to becoming young adults and to approaching middle and old age. When she accomplished something, performed on stage, or just gave any positive signs of maturing, my heart swelled with pride!

My sister Maggie, or MM, whose real name is Magdalina, named after one of my father's younger sisters in the Philippines, was born on my birthday. As a matter of fact she was born at the very hour my first birthday party was held. She came so quickly, she was born before they could get my mother to Columbia Hospital for Women, the same hospital where I was born. So she was delivered by my father, and permanently colored his new white suit an off-pink color.

It has been almost like having a twin—we told people we were year-apart twins. But despite being that close in age, there was never any question about who is the older sister, something she reminds me of, especially now that we are in our fifties.

We looked so very much alike, talked and walked and even dressed alike, which added to the illusion of being twins. Yet, I was always at least six inches taller than MM, and decidedly larger-framed.

We baffled people about our nationality too. Some days we passed for Indians—both Eastern and Native American. Other days we were seen as Hawaiians.

On one occasion, we tagged along with Dad while he filled out some paperwork for Catholic Charities on Massachusetts Avenue. We were painfully bashful and would not speak when spoken to. People could rarely break through Dad's accent to understand him,

The social workers whispered among themselves and tried to remember some Spanish phrases to help him to complete the paperwork, to help pull us out of our shells. We sat, unresponsive and hiding behind Dad, not uttering a word, further convinced them we did not know English. Out on the street we giggled and felt victorious for pulling off our fresh-off-the-boat immigrant performance.

MM was a year younger than everyone in Group One because she was just in kindergarten when we went to St. Vincent's. She missed Aunt Edna so much she used to cry herself to sleep. The first year we were there, MM got very thin, so thin Sister gave her milkshakes to fatten her up.

She also was a bed wetter and usually soaked through the sheets and the white wool Navy blanket and all the way down to the dark brown rubber pad that covered each bed just for this purpose. We all had to make our bed up each morning, despite how little we were. And you became progressively more responsible with each passing year for making the bed tidy, without wrinkles and with honest-to-God hospital corners.

The punishment MM received for wetting her bed was to strip the bed down and put on clean sheets without help from anyone. She always looked so little and so uncoordinated, stretching across the high bed trying to tuck the sheets in and smooth them out, folding the top sheet over the blanket.

It looked to me like she was being tortured one day. It was a Saturday morning. I remember this because we were getting ready to do heavier cleaning and chores—our "Saturday Duty." I came into the baby dormitory, the dorm for the youngest girls, and witnessed a horrific scene—one that brings tear to my eyes to this day.

Sister had put MM's wet panties over my little sister's head, crotch in her face, and the other girls were taunting her in a circle, like Little Sally Ann, sittin' in the sand:

"Magdalina Mondoñedo wet her pants!"

I felt so angry but so helpless to do anything. When Sister saw me she took the panties off her head, scolded MM and dismissed the other girls to the playroom. I hated Sister at that moment. How could she have been so cruel to my sister. She was poorly trained and did not have a real knack for dealing with the girls.

In her later years, however, this same Sister redeemed herself in my eyes in so many ways, while I was a teenager at St. Vincent's. She demonstrated a life utterly devoted to Christ and His children.

It bothered me that no one ever tried to figure out why MM wet the bed. There were no physical or psychological examinations or social workers visits that could uncover the reason for bedwetting or her occasional outbursts of rage. No one got to the root of the real problem, a problem she shared with me, but a problem I was helpless to handle myself. There just was no solution. No one would believe me either. So we told no one.

I think they just assumed that "she was exhibiting bad behavior," a term I learned from a report I read in the office about someone else's behavioral episodes. She always seemed to be in trouble. I tried protecting her and making excuses for her. They seemed to have no understanding of what was going on in her little head. Well, usually, I didn't either. She was quite complicated. She felt the same about me. I remember one Sister saying we were both impudent!

When we were in the "baby group" we took nightly baths in one of the old bathtubs that had the claw feet. We usually had the help of a few older girls, and of course Miss Nora. Miss Nora was a paid employee who helped Sister with the hundreds of chores it took to care for 20 or more little girls in the first or second grade. MM recalls a clean towel and fresh water being run for every third girl and she learned where to stand in line just as soon as she knew how to count to three so she would always get clean water. The details of this escaped me since I hated taking baths in this huge lavatory complex that reeked of fresh homemade lye soap! It never made any difference to me whether we did or didn't get the chlorine from the swimming pool off our skin every day. Perhaps I blocked out the experience entirely.

MM was the center of attention for still another strange event. I came into her dormitory and found the workmen, Mr. Sam, Mr. Boykins and Mr. Gene all gathered around her bed, trying to calm her screams and help her. It seemed she had pushed her head through the iron bars on her bed and couldn't get her head back out. They tried a number of different things to get her head out of the bars, including dabbing her with *Crisco* from a can, but nothing worked.

They eventually sawed the bars off to release her. Everyone in the group called her stupid, including myself, and kept asking her why she did this. I wondered too.

Years later she told me "I was just trying to escape to get back home—back to Aunt Edna's." I think we must have seen *The Wizard of Oz* too many times that year. We were always, as Sister complained, too sensitive and a bit on the dramatic side.

Miss Betty, the cook, whose face was a beautiful chestnut color, had apparently heard stories about the little Filipina sisters who were scared that the swimming pool would "eat them up." And now there was all this commotion in the baby dormitory with the younger sister getting her head stuck in the bars. We were never high on her list of favorite girls at St. Vincent's.

She didn't see what all of the fuss was about that first summer we came to St. Vincent's. "There are already two Filipina girls here." They were Alicia and Cora Panganiban. "These two ain't even half as dark as the four little colored sisters that just got here." She was referring to four sisters who were in Group One with us.

No one argued with Miss Betty. No one was about to have a discussion of racial issues with her. All you could say was *"uh huh"* the same way she would say uh huh when she was trying to block out someone's words that she did not agree with, while under the pretense of trying to be polite.

MM had one of everything before I did. A hula hoop, a pair of wooden-wheeled boot roller skates for the skating rink, a *Brownie* camera, a Japanese doll with a porcelain face, a play kitchen stove. Her "pitiful" act, the one she used for sympathy on everyone we met, got her lots of material goods, long before I even had an interest in acquiring such items. One item I coveted, however, was a cast iron toy bank, about 12 inches high, that opened at the top. I could not understand why she, younger than I, should have this treasure before me.

Foolishly, I tried to "get one up" on her with my ability to send *real* mail. I always had lots of stationery and stamps which I bought at the Valley Vista Pharmacy on Ashmead Place where Dad worked. Subsequently I ordered lots of important material in the mail—seeds, foreign stamps, books, shoe polish and the like.

Airmail was very special. It cost more to send. You had to purchase separate stamps just for this purpose. The rationale was that mail was generally delivered by train, so mail delivered by airplane, a new and more expensive mode of transportation, should cost more. Thin, onionskin writing paper and envelopes were sold everywhere.

Through my "junk mail" hobby, I was able to receive a piece of correspondence via "airmail" years before MM.

Miss Nora, whose private room was just off of the baby lavatory, was one of the most patient ladies we knew. She always asked us about our activities at school, she played games with us at home, she helped us with our homework at night and sometimes read stories to us before bedtime.

She had us fetch a glass of water every Sunday before she did our finger curls. Twenty little girls, at least 10 curls apiece, one glass and one long black comb, wetting down each head of hair, twirling the strands of hair around her forefinger to create each little finger curl. A lot of work for one elderly lady, but she proudly turned out 20 little Shirley Temple wanna-be's! Miss Nora was about as rotund as our Aunt Edna when she was pregnant. She was just as huggable, but we were just a bit standoffish because Miss Nora had a brace on one of her legs, shorter since birth, which made us just a little ill at ease. You could usually hear Sister coming down a hallway before you saw her because the beads from her two-inch long rosary would clang together, announcing her arrival on the scene. But Miss Nora's leg brace gave off a much louder warning. She had one leg shorter than the other and wore one stacked shoe to even them off. The brace was on the shorter side.

MM ran away several times. She snuck out the back gate and walked down Edgewood Street toward the streetcar stop. There was a bus stop that was much closer to St. Vincent's but she didn't want anyone to see her waiting there. So she went several blocks farther, to Fourth and Rhode Island Avenue, to the streetcar stop, always losing her nerve and coming back in the front gate and back up the front hill.

So much for all that practice. She went through with it once. In reality, she actually left one day, took a streetcar toward downtown, and ended up on New Jersey Avenue near Union Station. This happened to be where Mr. Sam picked up the films for our Friday-night movies in the auditorium. He spotted her just walking around, put her in his truck and took her back to St. Vincent's. No one ever knew what she had done. Mr. Sam was a gentleman. He never said a word about her great escape.

My little sister was like the *Great Houdini*—always escaping from injury. How she escaped from injury when getting her arm stuck in the wringer washing machine is pretty remarkable too. MM was growing up quickly and watched Sister Alma use the old wringer washing machine in the basement many times. She was so curious she had to figure out how the wringer squeezed the water out of the clothing. So she put her hand through the rollers to find out how it worked. It jammed. Sister Alma came to rescue her and heard some new prayers, new "litanies of the saints" and new commands for sending people to heaven, hell and purgatory. Well, let's just say MM chose some very bright and colorful words and Sister's washing machine was on a light and delicate setting!

Mr. Gene, a man we considered very old, worked in the boiler room. He was always there to mend things and to get us out of jams with Sister when we were destructive with our toys and other things around St. Vincent's. Equipping her with master skate keys and pliers, Mr. Gene put MM to work many times. He paid her two cents for each pair of skates she managed to put back together from the hundreds of ballbearing skate parts he kept in baskets in the boiler room. Considering a pickle cost a nickel at the DGS, MM was a wealthy girl from a few minutes of hard work.

In Sister Maria's group, when we were nine and ten years old, we put on a play—a spoof on the story of *Alice in Wonderland*. MM played the Queen of Hearts and I played Alice. We studied our parts, taking our roles quite seriously, perhaps too seriously. One of MM's lines was a command. She was supposed to glare at me and say, "Off with her head."

Just before the play was to be given MM and I had one of those nasty, familiar knock-down-drag-out sibling arguments, and she was still mad at me. When she delivered her lines for the performance, she swung her scepter around her head the way you would twirl a baton. She yelled, "Off with her head, off with her head, off with everybody's head." Then she bopped me on the head, put her hands on her hips mockingly and shouted at the top of her lungs, "So there!" She received the greatest applause from an audience who had no idea she had improvised. She got her personal relief. It was a turn of events and the argument was definitely over.

MM irritated me sometimes to the point of pulling my own hair and throwing myself in the looney bins at St. Elizabeth's. But I could not stay mad at her for long. She would stare me down till I told her everything was all right. I had best friends throughout the years— Yvette Yonkers, Mary Elisabeth AKA *Lizzie-Mike-Shirley-in-the-Springtime* Holmes, Jamie. But MM was my own little sister, and that put her in a special place in my heart always.

When we visited our Dad or Aunt on the weekends, we would have some very depressing moments during the course of the visit. We wished things could be normal. We wished we could have a family like everyone else. Always asking the question why? Why weren't we home with our family? Why did our mother have to drink? Why couldn't she take care of us?

We wanted what we lacked most—the closeness and security and love that parents give their children. We wanted the intimacy, we wanted to press up next to someone and hear their heartbeat when they told you that you were their little angel.

Inevitably we would sleep in the same room when we went on these overnights, and sometime in the middle of the night, we would get into the same bed. One Christmas Eve night, which we spent at St. Vincent's, MM could not sleep, worried that Santa Claus would not stop at St. Vincent's. In my wisdom, being a whole year older than MM, I assured her, "St. Vincent's is up on a hill so we will be easy to find. Santa Claus is pron the way."

Both at St. Vincent's and at home, MM and I had a very strange ritual, which we called *Putting the bedclothes around.* For whatever reason, we filled our emptiness by spreading out our old, worn-out clothes around us, tucking them in above our heads, at our feet, completely surrounding our bodies, as we slept. A strange substitute for real love, no doubt. It was comforting. We were encircled in what felt to us like the warmth and familiarity of our parents' embracing arms.

More Sisters

We watched her a hundred times. Turn on the light, place the fabric under the treadle, lower the foot, turn the wheel to get the needle into the fabric, then push down on the pedal with your knee against the treadle to make the Singer go. I begged Sister Maria to let me use the sewing machine to make myself a handmade dancing doll. I think the idea came from a Fred Astaire movie in which he tapdanced with a plastic blow-up doll.

My idea was to have a dancing partner whenever I wanted to do a waltz or a jitterbug. So I was going to make a life-sized doll that would hook on to me at the wrists and feet with strips of elastic.

I saved 30 cents and bought two packages of elastic from Stanley's down the street from St. Vincent's, but was unable to buy a package of ric-rac for decoration because I just didn't have another dime. The elastic, the old tattered sheet my Dad found for me, and a bunch of old towels I found in the arts and crafts room were the only materials I thought I needed.

Sister Maria would just have to loan me the sewing machine so I could sew it together. So I started my project and was determined to finish it all in one day. I doubled over the sheet once, laid down on the sheet and had my friend Mary Elisabeth trace my silhouette onto the sheet with a black laundry marker we took from Sister's desk. I found Sister's sewing scissors, which were marked indelibly with her name in black ink around a little never-ending piece of white fabric slipped through the finger loop. No one in their right mind would steal these scissors. With them marked so clearly, surely stealing them would be a mortal sin.

I cut the towels into shreds, cut the fabric pieces and pinned them together with straight pins from her pin cushion. Another girl said she watched her grandmother make a dress from a pattern and we should iron the pieces out before we sewed them. So we plugged in the iron which sat on the ironing board. Of course it was not supposed to be touched.

Nothing was premeditated. The next crime was pure and total impulse. Yvette Yonkers thought that since we had the iron turned on, it would be a good day for grilled cheese sandwiches! Yep, so in this very short period of time when Sister was in the chapel, Yvette and I slipped down to the kitchen and she boldly told the cook that Sister Maria wanted to give us an afternoon snack because we had been so good—she said Sister wanted the ingredients for grilled cheese sandwiches.

Miss Emma growled at Yvette but turned over a whole loaf of Wonder Bread, a huge stack of cheese slices and snapped, "You don't need no oleo, just gave you some last week." We ran back upstairs like the little thieves that we were, faster than we normally ran up the two flights of steps and got back to the sewing room where several greedy little girls were waiting anxiously.

None of us knew anything about the kitchen or cooking but we considered this loot a great treasure. We got busy with the sandwiches, making sure the iron was not too hot. It worked well. In between sandwiches we used a scouring pad just like Sister did when there was too much starch stuck on the iron. We were brilliant. We inhaled the sandwiches! But we ended up throwing half of them away because we could hear the rustling of Sister's cornette and the clattering of her noisy rosary beads coming down the hallway.

My sewing project was put on hold a while. Again I asked Sister if I could use the sewing machine. She was impressed when I showed her my cut-out pieces but she still scolded me for using the pins and scissors. She said she would sew it for me, but being thoroughly obstinate and contrary, I insisted I do it by myself. So we were at another standoff.

The next afternoon when Sister went to chapel, I stuffed my doll and pinned the pieces together with Sister's straight pins. Voila! It was done. Sewing machine or no sewing machine, it was put together. There were enough safety pins to hold it together, but instead I arranged the safety pins in a chain. I knew how long it would take to unpin three feet of chained safety pins. This idea was not unique; Sister had spent many an hour undoing pins that girls had chained together before my time

But that evening, out for revenge, since she wouldn't let me use the sewing machine, I put the doll on a chair in the sewing room. As far as I was concerned it was finished. Not machine sewn, just pinned together. At a glance you could not tell it was not sewn together. Still, I prayed that Sister would pick it up and get stuck from the hundreds of pins I had used.

Revenge is ugly. Just before we all fell off to sleep, Sister walked in her familiar graceful style to my bedside, gently placed the doll on the chair next to my bed, leaned over and whispered "You did a nice job putting your doll together. Be careful not to get stuck by the pins." She was not angry.

When she got back into her cell, there was a ripple of giggles in the dormitory. I was stunned. My anger was gone. How could you stay angry at her. I often wondered if she ever knew about the grilled cheese sandwiches that we cooked on the iron. Once again she proved herself to be beautiful to me as she did so many times before that.

It was Sister Maria who tried to transform our five o'clock supper into a formal dinner. She let us turn the horrid overhead fluorescent lights off and light some candles. And we could add special items, things that we bought with our own money from our "book." Our "book" was Sister's accounting system; she kept a running balance of our personal spending money in a small spiral notebook. With the money from our book we could have pickles, sticks of real butter in a butter dish or any other food item of "luxury."

Each table sat four girls, so it was important who was assigned to each table. Someone at my table brought in real glass goblets so for our Thursday evening formal dinner we did away with our cheap, made-in-Japan, plastic tumblers.

It was a challenge to go to Safeway and find what you wanted since you never had more than a quarter at any given time. Once I got a can of Campbell's baked beans that were not much of a formal dinner item and had to be eaten cold from the can. But it was the idea that we had something we purchased and added to the feast and they were delicious because they were eaten under candlelight.

MM and I turned nine and ten years old in Sister Maria's group. That year no one remembered our birthday all day so it was comforting to have one another, at least, to exchange birthday sentiments, even without the birthday gifts we had expected. But by dinner time we were pouting about the insensitivity of the rest of the group and especially Sister.

We were pleased after dinner that she had kept the secret. Dad showed up with a huge birthday cake and raspberry ice cream from Avignon Freres Bakery on Columbia Road. It was the best in the city! It was our best birthday.

In the dining room there was a large table with a lace table cloth on it. In the center was a bisque statue of Blessed Mother. Two of the girls had a little race around the table, pulled at the cloth, and the statue landed on the floor. Sister scolded the girls and told them, "The special statue was priceless." Reminiscing about the story, Sister said that later she heard some other girl telling the group, "And Sister said that statue was worthless!"

At night, just minutes after she turned off the horrid overhead fluorescent lights, Sister would come around the dormitory checking to see that we were okay. She would very gently pull your arms out from under your blankets and rest them on top of your body. She heard us giggling one night because one girl was talking in her sleep! Sister came out of her cell and without a word sprinkled holy water on her. It was kind of like a scaled-down exorcism!

Sister Maria was beautiful. Everyone said so. Dad said you could tell she must been a beautiful young girl before she went into the convent. She had thick black eyebrows and ivory colored skin. Maybe she was Italian or French. Lots of times while playing in the Grove I'd look at the beautiful statues of the Blessed Mother of Jesus and think about Sister Maria and the similarities.

I think she must have loved us as much as Mary loved her son

Jesus. I often prayed most sincerely that I could be as beautiful and kind and serene as Sister Maria when I grew up. She was so caring and intelligent and the epitome of beauty. She was what we all thought angels are like. Yes, we all considered Sister Maria to be beautiful.

Sister Maria had a spectacular view of the grounds from her bedroom window. Like a prayer, her words were poetic and graceful. She remarked so many times that she was "Blessed to be able to share this beautiful home with the Sisters, to contemplate the works of the Blessed Virgin Mary, and to care for God's little children at St. Vincent's."

In earlier days, the Daughters of Charity who did not serve in other capacities, but were the supervisors of the children when the children were not in school were called "Angels." How very fitting.

Equally beautiful as Sister Maria, with eyebrows just as dark, but much bushier, framing a round chubby face and kissed with sparkling, playful Irish eyes, Sister Alma was the spirit of St. Vincent's during the 1950s and 1960s. Sister Alma could sing. Sister Alma could laugh. Sister Alma had hay fever and when she sneezed you could hear her almost to the corner of Fourth and Rhode Island Avenue!

Sister Alma was full of little ditties. She could ad lib stories, specializing in the ones that started, "There once was a black-haired little 10-year-old girl with a long ponytail and freckles" and ended with some great moral. She could make up songs on the spot to match the situation. And it was eerie when she would almost read your mind. You never wanted to do anything wrong because she might laugh out loud and tell you that you could have been more clever than she, and that maybe you could have outwitted her.

There was a lady named Betty who lived at 4th and Channing Streets. She had cerebral palsy and had problems speaking clearly. Sister Alma would visit Betty often. Betty lay stretched out on a recliner on her front porch and would wave and yell at the children as they called out to her. We were a little uncomfortable the closer we got to her house. But Sister urged us to visit Betty when we could, telling us that by some strange fate, Betty had been afflicted with a disease that could have happened to any of us. Betty would clutch your hand with a grip like a lady wrestler and her mother had to pry her long pale white fingers off our scrawny little digits.

Betty was not dangerous and she seemed to enjoy our visits. After some time, we looked forward to seeing her. Sister's gentle treatment toward Betty helped us overcome some of the fear we initially had. We knew that Betty was a Child of God just like us. Sister was patient with us, which was difficult at times. We were, in turn, a lot more understanding of Betty's condition and some other disabilities. It is not unrealistic to say that Betty might be watching and waving at us from another world.

Just before bedtime Sister Alma used to use a little pocket knife to cut off and give you a little sliver of Camphor Ice for your chapped lips. She had a wonderful New England accent and would recite:

> "'God bless us and save us,' said Mrs. O'Davis
> As she fell down the stairs with a sack of potatoes.
> You say to-may-toes, I say to-mah-toes
> You say po-tay-toes, I say po-tah-toes.
> To-may-toes, to-mah-toes, po-tay-toes, po-tah-toes.
> Let's call the whole thing off."

We thought she made it up. She could have. It was very Sister Alma-ish!

There were banisters in the building that went along the sides of the slate steps from the attic to the third floor, and all the way to the basement. Along the steps was a slick, smooth ledge of slate that always seemed to call out to us, "Slide on me." Sister was constantly telling us *not* to slide down the banisters on your bottom or glide down the ledge on foot.

But lo and behold. There was Sister Alma one day, hiking up her habit, exposing her black stockings and her thick two-inch heeled orthopedic-looking shoes. Her right foot on the ledge, she leaned into the wall like Sonja Henne, the skater, on ice and slid down. An agile ten-year-old could only slide down the slate ledge the distance of five or six steps without killing herself. Sister's slick oxfords took her down almost half a flight of stairs and then, BOOM, she crashed!

She stumbled then landed smack on her bottom. Her habit flew up higher to expose her chubby thighs and she just sat in shock, but she was okay. Then she saw us. Any other nun would have campused us for a month just for being there and witnessing the sight. Not Sister Alma. She bent forward with joy and just roared like someone was tickling her, exceeding the usual decibels of her Glen-Echo laughing lady cackle.

When she finally stopped laughing, she gathered herself up, recouped her dignity, looking up the stairs at us and said something about verifying that the steps were indeed too dangerous for us to slide down. When she winked and hurried off, we knew we were safe and there would be no consequences for witnessing this scene.

Still we were embarrassed even if she had glossed over the incident. It was as eye-opening as seeing the Sisters eat a meal in front of you. This was just never done before Vatican II.

When MM was in the fourth grade at St. Anthony's Grade School there was a boy in her class who was always giving her a hard time and frightened her. One day MM came home in tears to Sister Alma. Sister counseled MM and told her that the boy was really a nice boy. How did she know that? And she gave MM advice on how to handle this little rascal. Sister Alma confessed to MM after almost 40 years, that the boy was none other than Sister Alma's dear sweet little nephew!

Sister Margaret, who stood about four feet zero, was European. No one knew anything about Sister Margaret as a younger nun. We only knew her as the very old nun who was older than dirt, who took care of the sisters' laundry. This was a very cumbersome job since the sisters had to starch the white cotton parts of their "habit."

The habit consisted of a navy-blue heavy wool fabric dress garment, heavy cotton in the summer and a stiff collar which came down the front of the chest and crisscrossed without the use of pins or buttons. As little girls with a growing curiosity about all things sexual, we were always amazed at the variation in breast and waistline sizes. The habit seemed to flatten out the breasts but some sisters' breasts were so large they couldn't be disguised. The amount of fabric used to go around a portly-built nun's behind, given the obvious requirement for a large size and the gathered style of the skirt, was enough to make a circus tent or at least a couple of good-sized tablecloths—definitely not a one-size-fits-all garment.

But with Sister Margaret in the laundry, located on the ground floor and away from the main activity of sisters and girls, the laundry was very much a one-sister-does-it-all operation. Actually, Sister Margaret should have had a sign over a jumbo-size laundry basket in her laundry room that read:

Sisters: Leave all dirty habits here!

But, alas, she did not have the same twisted sense of humor as the rest of us at St. Vincent's!

The white cornette headdress and collar were amazing works of art and had to be carefully laundered. This tested Sister Margaret's patience. After running them through the washing machine they were heavily starched and placed on metal forms to dry—a very precise science to assure the perfect amount of stiffness. Catherine DeForge used to stick her hands down in the hot starch to mix the solution well. She was always reminded,"There should be no bubbles" when the collars and cornettes were laid out flat to dry.

We visited the laundry often, in Sister Margaret's absence of course, for she was not known for being patient, nor accommodating to a curious, wandering girl. She had very little help with the Sisters' laundry. Occasionally Bill Marean's wife, Marie would help. And Jamie and MM were "assigned" to her often.

What possessed me one day to toy with her laundry escapes me now. But I remember being driven one day to mischief. After filling her king-size Pepsi bottle with water and replacing the cork cap with holes for sprinkling back in the bottle's neck—a 1950s style substitute for a spray bottle for spraying clothing before ironing—I selectively applied big gobs of water to the tips of the cornettes only.

Walking around the laundry was like being in a factory where armor was made. It conjured up views of Robin Hood unhooking suits of armor and little flexible human beings climbing out of the piles of metal and steel, being released from the stiffening pain. I just wanted to set the cornettes free. It might have actually been a blessing to ease the pain in the collars because the sisters, never complaining but sometimes wincing from the discomfort, always seemed to have a severe pain in the neck. Nevertheless, only the cornettes that resembled white birds were wet down with the water.

No one saw me. No one knew what I had done. And I never heard a word said about the incident, not from the sisters nor the girls. The only evidence of my crime showed itself in the next several weeks at random times. Sister Elizabeth answering the telephone in the office, Sister Maria going up to the Communion rail in the chapel, and Sister Alma serving us hot dogs and beans in the Grove—all suffered the droopy "wing tips." And me—suffering more because I could not crack a smile or laugh out loud for fear of being found out. I couldn't let on that I knew anything about this or have any pleasure in the outcome or I'd be starched myself.

I internalized my guilt for months after this, never knowing quite how to confess this sin to Father Adler in confession; was it a "mortal" or "venial" sin? I did not know which Commandment I had broken. It seemed like a toss-up between the 4th—*Honor Thy Father and Thy Mother*, and the 9th—*Thou shalt not covet they neighbor's goods.*

Sister Margaret was also known for helping girls make doll clothing in the two craft rooms just outside of her laundry. MM and I made the figurines for a complete Nativity scene from plaster of Paris. One room was used for all kinds of crafts using potholder loops, plastic gimp for making skate key chains, paper, papier mache, clay and beads, etc. The other room was used for sewing and embroidery projects.

Sister Cecilia was the Superior when MM and I came to live at St. Vincent's in 1952; she remained there until 1958. To a six-year-old child, she was frightening, dictatorial and overbearing. I thought maybe the wire-rimmed glasses she wore pinched her nose too tightly. And I was sure there were horns on her head, held down by the cornette.

But I soon learned that to rule the world at St. Vincent's—an administration of a 300-foot wide building—an huge institution on 19 acres of land, almost 100 girls, a dozen or more assigned or visiting nuns, and a large staff of employees of every kind—for this world Sister Cecilia was perfect.

We also found out she had a softer side and even asked us for our opinions on how to improve the operation at St. Vincent's. She just chuckled when I suggested that we keep the pool open for ice skating in the winter, and that the groups be mixed with girls of all ages so that it was more like a regular home. She said I sounded like I was preparing to be a social worker.

Once she actually played a guessing game with us, pretending she was a gypsy with a crystal ball. We asked her the question, "What will I be when I grow up?" Sister would predict the answer. I told her that I must have had a religious vocation because "No matter how much my brown scapular itches, I can take it." Sister said I would never survive in the convent because I thought rules were meant to be broken. We didn't see her often but she seemed to understand us well.

Sister Serena was the Superior just before Sister Cecilia. I didn't know her as a child but remembered the older girls raving on about how wonderful she was and how well she treated them. She was known to play the organ in chapel and she had a superior memory for retaining all of the facts of stories from many generations of girls who lived at St. Vincent's.

The word *charismatic* which described President Kennedy in the 1960s described Sister Serena. Even her name represented her personality—tranquil, calm, serene.

Sister Bernard on the other hand I knew extremely well because when I returned in high school, I was in her "Seton Group." Tall, slender, angular, full of nervous energy. Sister Bernard was like a Mama Bear with her "cubs;" no one could harm us. No one fought harder for us, got more material goods for us and found meaningful, seemingly normal, activities for our enjoyment. There is more information on Sister Bernard in a later chapter of this book.

Sister Mary Frances was the "show biz" nun. If an occasion presented itself to show off some music or dancing ability, you can just bet that Sister Mary Frances was behind the scenes. Hope Baza remembers Sister playing ping pong and jacks with the girls. And she would read *Little Women* to them at bedtime. There is more information on Sister Mary Frances in the chapter of this book entitled "Putting on a Show."

Having all of these Sisters protect and guide us was like living back at Aunt Edna's with all of the aunts, uncles and other relatives in the same house and in the same neighborhood. If you screwed up at school they knew it. If you got special recognition at school they also knew it. If you needed protection from a bully at school you could be sure you'd get the moral support you needed, even a quick lesson in self-defense from a visiting Sister!

And whenever you were depressed, the feedback from the Daughters of Charity could run the gamut from a simple pat on the shoulder with a quick "Oh cheer up!" to acting out a pantomine of playing a violin with a bow, all the way up to a quote from the Holy Bible that reminded you just how trivial your problem might be and how cherished you were.

"The Lord is my rock, my fortress, and my Savior;
My God is my rock, in whom I find protection.
He is my shield, the strength of my salvation,
and my stronghold, my high tower,
my Savior, the one who saves me from violence.
I will call on the Lord, who is worthy of praise,
for He saves me from my enemies."
(2 Samuel 22:4).

We were certainly privileged to received these profound reminders that strengthened and sustained us. These reminders were not given with a warm, blanketing embrace. They were more like protective coats of armor!

A Father, a Mentor, a Friend

If the Sisters were the *heart* of our home, Father Edward Adler was surely the *soul* of St. Vincent's, and without a doubt, the holiest man any of us had ever known. It seems he was always there as the chaplain through many generations, whether one refers to the ladies who lived at St. Vincent's in the 1940s, 1950s or 1960s.

Every morning he walked about four blocks to St. Vincent's from the Redemptorist House, his religious order located on Seventh Street, to say the six o'clock Mass. He was there again for the seven a.m. Mass on Sundays, and Benediction and confessions on Friday evenings.

Years before my sister and I came to live at the home, Father Adler used to drive the girls to summer camp in Maryland, even taking them for boat rides on the bay and a once-a-week trip to the beach. He was an avid photographer, always sticking a light meter in front of your nose and clicking away on his camera. He made you feel so special, like you were a celebrity or a fashion model. Father's photographs were wonderful and he was always making extra prints for our albums. He created a priceless photo history of St. Vincent's over the years.

Father Adler kept himself very trim, probably from his robust lifestyle, walking to St. Vincent's every morning, rain, snow or shine, and gardening to keep up our green pepper supply. He wore suspenders when he was casually dressed, and he removed his Roman collar. But he always seemed to wear his crisp fedora hat placed carefully on his head. He sometimes walked around with a corncob or a heavier, bent wooden pipe that carried the sweetest-smelling cherry tobacco. He must have just liked the taste of the pipe because we never saw him light it up.

You always knew when he was around—you would hear the jingle of coins being thrown down a long hallway or into the pool, followed by a band of screaming girls trying to catch the pennies he had tossed. One day he approached a high school girl, Frances O'Malley, who of course, did not chase after the pennies. He placed a gorgeous, fragrant white magnolia flower in full bloom surrounded by the most beautiful green leaves into her extended hands and said, "You are a young lady, and this is for you." She was so touched. Frances, who was sixteen years old, felt this was the first acknowledgment of her femininity. Needless to say, she walked a little taller and straighter from then on.

Father Adler liked to work in his garden and he would hide green peppers or an occasional ripe tomato or two, in the bushes along the back driveway. What a refreshing, unexpected treat it was to crunch into a juicy, fleshy green pepper or a juice-down-your-arms ripe tomato!

One year I bought carrot, radish and watermelon seeds from the Brookland Hardware Store and planted them on the 15th of March according to the directions on the back of the packet, in a small plot along the fence in the Grove that was rarely used. Father Adler checked out the plot from time to time, offering advice and helping to weed the garden.

To my surprise, despite the dogs from the neighborhood getting into everything, and the little kids in Group One pulling up a leaf or two, everything grew. The carrots and radishes were scrumptious and were ready early in the summer, while the watermelon vines continued to grow and climb everywhere, forecasting a potentially bumper crop.

One morning it was over. The watermelon vines had been pulled out of the ground and lay in the grass half shriveled from lack of water. So angry was I that I carried them into the house, ran into the chapel and placed them on the steps of the altar. Father Adler came into the chapel calmly and quietly blessed the vines. He said in a whisper "if we were Jewish, I would be doing this all of the time."

Years before we came to St. Vincent's, Father Adler had a "victory garden" near the back gate. He gave some of the produce he grew to the girls and for the Redemptorist priests where he lived, but he said the garden was "for the poor."

Father Adler was very knowledgeable about birds too. There were hundreds of different species in the Grove of St. Vincent's. He made himself available to point out to a curious little girl which were the woodpeckers, and what their job was in life. There was a bothersome woodpecker who pecked away at a tall tree near the back gate.

He remarked, one day, when the woodpecker was especially industrious, "Should we charge him rent to live in that tree?" We sat for some time listening to the Bob White birds, trying our best to imitate the whistle following Father Adler's lead. He tested us once and asked, "Is that a Bob White? Of course we knew it was. But he informed us, "That's Bob White's mother calling him to dinner!"

Father Adler seemed to know a lot about the great outdoors and that evil weed that lurked behind every giant tree around the property of St. Vincent's—Poison Ivy! And as many times as he told me, "Beware of the shiny leaves," holding poison ivy and oak leaves in his bare hands, I never learned. He even marked the bushes with bright red ribbons so we knew to avoid those areas. Still, I was becoming known as the "poison ivy kid."

One summer when I was about nine years old I was confined to an infirmary that had been created just for me. It was on the third floor of the house. It isolated me, in my "possibly contagious" state, from the other girls. Father Adler came to visit me. He took a picture of my grotesquely swollen face and leg, and tied a huge red ribbon around my swollen knee.

I had been so self-conscious of my appearance I did not even want my sister to come to visit me. But I knew I would feel better after Father Adler's visit. I had read a story about Father Damien and the lepers of Molokoi. It felt the same. I was isolated on my little island and I was an untouchable. I knew he would not be repulsed by my appearance, and I was happy when he showed up in a few days with my newly developed photographs. Since the swelling had gone down a bit, I could enjoy the pictures and finally laugh at myself.

All priests swear to keep what is heard in confession confidential, and we never doubted that Father Adler would defend this to his death. We certainly gave him a lot to defend over the years. At school, confessions were heard once a month; home, at St. Vincent's we went to Father Adler once a week. I always confessed my venial sins at school and saved my mortal sins for Father Adler. Not that the penance he gave you was easier, for it rarely was. And I was not afraid that I would shock the priest at school, for I knew too many people before me had confessed a whole multitude of sins and transgressions. I just felt that Father Adler knew me well and I would have to be absolutely honest with him and therefore have complete remorse for my sins.

He would slide the dreaded wooden shutter open to expose the light to your side of the confessional when it was your turn. The confessional shutter on Father's other side was closed off for privacy. I counted on that.

His strong profile with the Roman nose was stately, yet comforting. You knew that the mesh screen that separated you about 18 inches from his face was quite transparent. And you knew that if he did not really see your face because you purposely twisted and bent your head in such as way as to not be noticed, he would recognize your voice anyway. So you could not hide.

Somehow you did not want to hide from Father Adler. Once I went to confession just to say, "I have no sins." I could sense the smile stretching across his mouth but he remained his usual poised self. He ignored what I said and prompted me, "Bless me father…." We went through the whole confessional ritual anyway, and I repeated at the appropriate time "Father, I have not sinned." For my penance he told me to pray for him.

"*Corpus Dómini nostri Jesu Christi custódiat ánimam tuam in vitam æterrnam.*"

You received the host on your tongue and said, "Amen" when Father Adler stood in front of you at the altar rail.

You would then pass the *paten*, the golden plate-like instrument for catching a fallen host, to the girl kneeling at your left at the Communion rail. We had no altar boys, so everyone responded to Father Adler's prayers. When we were not in a group setting, one of the Sisters or a high school girl would "serve," the Mass by these responses.

I made my first Holy Communion at St. Peter's Church on Capitol Hill with my second-grade classmates from school, complete with a frilly white dress and flowing veil for my head. Dad bought me the "First Holy Communion Kit" that contained the veil the prayer book made of mother-of-pearl and the white rosary beads. The boys' kits had a black prayer book and rosary beads. There was a blue tie instead of a veil. We felt like little brides. I was hoping to get my picture taken with Paul Massey or Jerry McSorley, two boys that I loved.

My mother, whom I had not seen in years, showed up. I was surprised at her boldness when she walked up to the Communion rail, winking at me as she passed, to receive the host. She was not Catholic. Couldn't imagine her asking for special permission to go to Communion. Couldn't imagine her making her "Easter duty," a mandatory confession and Communion, required of Catholics once a year. But my Communion did not "take" in my mind until I went to the altar at St. Vincent's the following Sunday and received the host from Father Adler.

Father Adler provided us with spiritual direction; he mentored us through his example. He was our chaplain for 27 years, our father, our friend.

Going to the Movies

Our auditorium was not large, maybe 40 feet by 80 feet, but it was the location of some of the grandest shows and festivities in Washington, D.C. Halloween parties, Christmas pageants, 35mm movies, St. Patrick's Day plays, ballet classes, even Cuban merengue parties! Something was going on in the auditorium all of the time.

Located directly underneath the Chapel, the auditorium could comfortably seat 60 to 75 people on folding wood chairs. For an area of this modest size, it had a respectably professional look, with a raised, three-foot high, wooden stage, as well as fully equipped backstage facilities, complete with interior and exterior purple velvet curtains hung the full length, floor to ceiling.

Every Friday night we were treated to a 35mm movie right there in our "family room"—our auditorium. Mr. Sam would pick up the movie reels from the distributor downtown, which had been carefully selected by the Superior, under the best advisement from movies listed under the Catholic Bishops' Legion of Decency.

The Legion of December was created in 1934 to stop the showing of immoral movies. Catholics were requested by the U.S. bishops to take a pledge in church to never go to any morally objectionable movie and to never go to any movie theater that had ever shown a morally objectionable film. This is the pledge.

"In the name of the Father and of the Son and of the Holy Ghost. Amen. I condemn all indecent and immoral motion pictures, and those which glorify crime or criminals. I promise to do all that I can to strengthen public opinion against the production of indecent and immoral films, and to unite with all who protest against them. I acknowledge my obligation to form a right conscience about pictures that are dangerous to my moral life. I pledge myself to remain away from them. I promise, further, to stay away altogether from places of amusement which show them as a matter of policy."

Films were rated
"A" that were *morally unobjectionable,*
"B" — *morally objectionable in part* and
"C" — *CONDEMNED.*

There were also sub-categories of "A" films, which further broke down the movies into three additional categories — A-1, A-2 and A-3. It was always vague in my mind what was actually meant by *morally objectionable.*

This rating list greatly reduced the number of movies available for us to watch. Sister chose the Friday evening movies, so we had no choice in the matter at home. But we were able to go to the local neighborhood movies — the Newton or the Village — on Sundays if we did not go home with our families.

Dad took us to the Newton Movie Theatre one Sunday, where we surprisingly did not run into any of the St. Vincent girls. We assumed they went to the Village Theatre instead. The movie was *The Man with the Golden Arm* starring Frank Sinatra.

MM and I then remembered that it was a "B" movie and Sister would not have allowed us to see it. We watched the newsreel, the usual two cartoons, and the *coming attractions* before the film, then we hunkered down in our seats with a big box of buttered popcorn, feeling rather self-satisfied that we had gotten-one-over on Sister. We were about to see our first "B" movie and she would never know. I loved Frank Sinatra and was looking forward to the main "attraction."

But before the credits had even finished rolling at the beginning of the film, my conscience was beginning to bother me. Like a scale weighing the good vs. the evil, there was the yummy, buttery popcorn and the "B" movie on one side and Sister's frown on the other. It mattered very little that it was wrong to see the movie. The vision of Sister's frown worked on my mind and finally won my mental debate.

I stood up and walked to the aisle, pleading with Dad and MM to leave the theatre with me. He could not understand what was so wrong about the movie. I tried everything. I told him I was sick. I told him it would be a mortal sin to watch the movie. Dad finally got up to avoid making a scene and MM followed defiantly.

Once we were outside on the street, I told Dad Sister would be upset with us. He agreed it was not good to watch the movie without any further argument. MM, gobbling down her popcorn contently, said it didn't matter to her that we were not going to see the movie because, "There's no one I can brag to. If I do tell anyone I saw a 'B' movie I'll be in big trouble."

There was one movie that I had to see that was probably given a rating of "A-3" or a "B." It was a Cinderella-type movie—*Daddy Long Legs* with Audrey Hepburn. She was a ward of a benefactor she had never met—Fred Astaire. He pays her way through boarding school and she writes him letters of appreciation and keeps him abreast of her activities. This movie had a very touching, romantic feel to it. In my wildest daydreams, I let my imagination run away with me and I often compared our experience at St. Vincent's to Audrey Hepburn's experience in a prestigious European boarding school.

How much more glamorous it would have been to have our own personal Daddy Long Legs write out checks for our tuition, room and board to a headmaster at our imagined, prestigious boarding school, than to have my Dad scrape for every hard-earned dollar to pay the Catholic Charities office, usually in crumpled well-worn bills, for my keep at St. Vincent's.

They showed *I was a Teenage Werewolf* one Sunday at the movies. MM and I did not go home with Dad that weekend. We joined the other girls at the Newton Theatre for what promised to be an exciting movie. We sat in the front row so we would not miss a thing. About 15 minutes into the movie, half the kids ran out of the movie house. It was just too scary. There was a stampede to get through the doors. We didn't want to get crushed, so all of the St. Vincent's girls ran into the girls bathroom, climbed on the partitions till we felt it was safe to come down.

I guess we had our share of climbing trees outside and partitions inside, so it was not a problem to reach the top of the partitions before the kids from the neighborhood could even figure out how to get up.

We didn't ask for our money back. No one remembered the details of the movie. We just kind of hung around the bathroom for another hour, then went back to our seats when the second film started. A St. Vincent's girl was not going to lose out on a double feature just because the first show wasn't to her liking!

There were also several 3-D movies shown at the Newton. You had to wear the specially made cardboard glasses with the little piece of pink plastic in the eye holes. These were great, because if the movie were too scary, you just yanked the glasses off till that scene was over. *The House of Wax* with Vincent Price gave us the heebie-jeebies, but no problem. Just remove your glasses and you would be fine till a scary scene had passed.

Occasionally MM and I would go downtown to the movies. The RKO Keith's and Loew's were all first-rate movie houses and could rationalize charging twice as much for their shows. But it was worth it. We saw the big shows, like *Ben Hur*, *The Ten Commandments* and *Gigi.*

One of my favorite movies was *Brigadoon* with Gene Kelly. When Gene Kelly and his buddy left Brigadoon to return to New York City, Brigadoon disappeared. Actually, it turned out that the people in the town would sleep for 100 years, then wake up as though it were the next day. Great fantasy!

MM and I fantasized that if we both ran away from St. Vincent's (she herself ran away many times), St. Vincent's would disappear. But if we then returned, the girls and Sisters would sleep for 100 years, just as in Brigadoon. It was very tempting to run away sometimes. But then, where we would have gone always became the big question we could not answer.

Movies continued to be the great way to escape from our problems, perfect for internalizing and fantasizing. When the movie *The Miracle* with Caroll Baker made its way to the big screen, I adopted the story as my own. The epic unfolds the story of Carroll Baker leaving the convent, having a fascinating "outside" life with great a affair that ends in tragedy, then her return to the convent and the subsequent miracle—rain finally comes to end a drought and a statue of the Blessed Mother is returned to a little village church. My sixteen-year-old imagination parralleled my pitiful life to the story of *The Miracle*. This may have been considered "sacriligious" in those days. I am certain that *The Miracle* set me up to wholeheartedly embrace *The Thornbirds* as my personal tale when it came to the screen in the 1980s. Movies are bliss!

Early School Daze

I attended kindergarten at St. Peter's School on Capitol Hill. When I entered St. Vincent's Orphanage in 1952, I continued school at St. Pete's in the first grade. MM had to attend St. Pete's too. Aunt Edna picked her up at school every day in kindergarten, and walked her back to school. Then she walked MM back to school at three o'clock so she could ride the bus with me to go back to St. Vincent's.

School was on the other side of town so we rode Capitol Transit to get there. There were some older girls who also attended St. Pete's, so they showed us the way on the bus, and most of the time we were chaperoned by them. There were no problems on the 45-minute trip to school that required a transfer of buses at the Archives Building, if we simply followed their lead.

One morning our *A-5, Fort Drum* bus detoured from its regular route and passed through different streets, streets totally foreign to us. We panicked. Fortunately, there was a regular passenger who knew our routine because he took the same route. He was the same man who possessed amazing dexterity in folding the *Washington Post* vertically, so that only the portion of the newspaper he was reading was exposed, the rest of the paper was folded out of view. He left himself wide open to sharing his paper, over his shoulder, to those who read as fast as he.

The tall lanky man with the huge paper-folding hands calmed us and showed us that the detour would still get us to St. Pete's. Trusting and vulnerable, we followed his lead. He saved the day.

There were two boys in my class that I loved. Totally smitten, I wanted to marry them both. Each of them had decided in the first grade, at a tender young age of six, that he was going to be a priest when he grew up. This was bad news for me. I would not be able to marry either one if their vocation interest in the priesthood continued.

Jerry McSorley lived in my neighborhood on South Carolina Avenue. One day when we were in kindergarten, he had lunch at our house and spent an afternoon playing hide-n-go-seek under the oak dining room table with the big claw feet. In between peeking down in the basement to see my cousin's Lionel layout with the hundreds of houses and animals—"hands off" to anyone under 10 years old—and opening and closing the oak pocket doors that separated the living and dining room, he tried impressing my Aunt with his amazing imitations of our pastor, Father Christopher of St. Peter's Church. He would imitate Father blessing us and saying Mass on our dining room table.

While my aunt was hanging clothes out back near the fig tree in the yard, Jerry and I snuck into the bathroom on the second floor of the house. Up to that point, I had never seen a boy's penis. My older cousin Ray never shut the door when he used the bathroom, so I might have had an opportunity or two. But I swear he peed with his dirty never-been-washed Navajo-print bathrobe on, so there was never a show for my curiosity.

Jerry said, "I'll show you mine, if you show me yours." We were curious. He went first. I peeked at him, then I ran downstairs to help Aunt Edna hang laundry.

Paul Massey, the other priest wannabe was just as human to me. In school, Sister would always chide him for having dirty fingernails. This was very typical of all of the altar boys at our school. Sister would harass him with comments like, "Would you want your grandmother receiving the Sacred Host from a priest that had nails as dirty as yours?" or something like "Good heavens, Paul. Your nails are so dirty you could plant potatoes in them." Never verbalizing these brainstorms, I used to think of those kinds of comments as "nunnisms." Paul called it "Sister on my back."

When I was a second grader, I won $5.00 in a jingle contest at school. This was an extremely large sum of money for a seven-year-old in those days. We were holding a carnival at St. Pete's with games, food and prizes for all eight grades. Our class was in charge of a fishing pond. You would take your fishing rod, which had a big hook on the end, lower it into the pond and try to hook it onto a plastic fish with a big loop on its back. We tried it out. It was pretty easy to hook a fish when you concentrated. But add a bunch of second-graders out of the classroom for the day and all hell broke loose. Hooks got all tangled, kids caught each other's uniforms on the hooks and water splashed everywhere. We knew the rest of the school would love it too and we were right. If you hooked a fish in the allotted time, you got to take home a real goldfish in a glass bowl.My winning jingle was chosen just a few days before the carnival. The slogan was short and sweet, and the words fit neatly on the flimsy white cardboard posters we decorated in class to advertise our money-making booth:

Make a wish. Catch a fish
And you'll be fond
Of the fish pond!

My prize money got me all kinds of "junk" from the DGS, District Grocery Store, the little grocery and convenience store by St. Vincent's—rolls of Necco wafers, bottles of Tru-Ade, packages of Lik-M-Aid, Hershey Bars, BB Bats, Mary Janes, ruby-red wax candy lips and other "penny candy" and jumbo dill pickles from the Yaffee's pickle vat! All this and I didn't even have to turn in soda bottles for the deposit money.

When I got home to St. Vincent's, Sister didn't believe my story about winning the money from the jingle contest. She saw all my loot. She wanted to know what I wrote, so I proudly recited it for her. There was no congratulatory message in her response. She said my jingle and my story were "far fetched." She made me share the goods with the other girls as our TV snack. There seemed to more than enough for everyone in the group.

The DGS employed a delivery man who drove around in a small white truck, transporting special-order items directly to the customers' homes in the neighborhood. He may have doubled as the butcher, we guessed, for he always donned a filthy, blood-stained white apron over his clothing. The rumor was that he could a spot a St. Vincent girl getting off the bus by herself and walking home to the back gate. His strategy was to wait till she passed the DGS store and was up Edgewood Street just far enough that there was no foot or street traffic, park his truck on the left side of the girl's pathway and lift his apron, exposing himself to her. No one was really traumatized by this display of his goods. But we knew we did not want to be around the area of the DGS when he was in sight. It was something we shared with the other girls once we got back into the gates of St. Vincent's.

To my knowledge, no one ever reported the DGS delivery man to Sister. We all just assumed she would not believe us. When you told such far-fetched tales, someone in authority might just assume that you are exaggerating and you were ready for St. Elizabeth's.

St. Elizabeth's, located in Southeast, was the home for the insane. You might survive being placed at Good Shepherd Home, for girls who might have broken the law or gotten pregnant. Maybe even the D.C. Receiving Home, another threatening placement. But never St. Elizabeth's. We heard stories about adults going there and never returning.

MM and I saw the pervert from the DGS many times, inside the store or just standing by his truck, wearing his apron on the outside of his coat and flashing a huge grin on his rugged unshaven face. We quickened our steps when we saw him, reaching a full run by the time we got to the back gates. Reports from the St. Vincent girls were probably never given to the Yaffee's, who owned the DGS. He could have been a close friend to the owners. One thing was for sure—we did not want to "make waves" and have our candy-buying privileges taken away at the DGS.

Archbishop Patrick O'Boyle came to St. Peter's Church and gave the Sacrament of Confirmation to hundreds of children. I was about in the fourth grade. As no one knew when he would be available again at our Church, the children came from several different classrooms and grades. We practiced the ritual for weeks at school, allowing someone, acting as the Bishop to ever so lightly "slap" your face, after you knelt to kiss his ring.

As is the tradition, we chose Confirmation names, usually saints whose lives we wished to emulate. I chose *Maria* for Maria Goretti, an Italian saint, the patron saint of purity. I liked the way the name *Maria* sounded with my other names. And I liked the fact that the name *Maria* could be Italian, Spanish, Polish—almost any ethnic group could claim this name. It certainly added a few more syllables to my name—Juanita Estifano Maria Mondoñedo.

MM chose *Mary* for the sinner Mary Magdalen, because she identified with the story of the repentant sinner, and because she didn't want her name any longer than it had to be. We firmly believed we had become "Soldiers of Christ" and we felt so holy at that time.

MM switched schools. She attended St. Martin's on North Capitol Street, which was much closer to St. Vincent's. After the older girls finished eighth grade and graduated from St. Peter's Grade School, I was the only one that still went across town on the bus to get to school. Going such a distance between home and school must have been too much for the nuns to worry about. So when I entered the fifth grade and MM, the fourth, we both switched schools and went to St. Anthony's Grade School in a neighborhood called *Brookland*.

Brookland, D.C. is said to be a "little Italy" because it has more Catholic institutions in its small area than anywhere else in the world except the Vatican.

We walked to St. Anthony's most of the time and took the bus when it rained or when the snow was too deep. Out the back gate, down Edgewood Street, past the DGS on the corner at Franklin Street and across the bridge at Franklin Street by Noyes School, then left down Twelfth to St. Anthony's. Coming home we would take an alternate route past the Vander Vossen's, the beautiful little tulip-laced house and yard, with the miniature windmill, quite famous in the neighborhood, at 10th Street, past the "circle house"—a circular house that looked like an enclosed merry-go-round, completely surrounded by a wooden porch, and finally a right hand turn at the Stone Straw Company to go over the Franklin Street Bridge that crossed over the B&O Railroad tracks that came north from Union Station.

At 8:38 a.m. on the 14th of January, 1953, the "Federal Express" train, making its way South from Boston, crashed into a wall at Union Station. The train had people who were traveling to Washington, D.C. for the first inauguration of President Eisenhower. The train had no brakes. It smashed through the stationmaster's office, demolished the main news stand and slid across the concourse toward the waiting room. The floor gave way and the "GG-1" and two other cars fell to the baggage room below. There were injuries but luckily no one was killed.

So as not to spoil the grand inaugural celebration, the two cars were removed the next day. GG-1 was left in the baggage room and a temporary floor was built over the locomotive. Three days after the accident, Union Station was re-opened.

Meanwhile up about a mile and a half north of the site of the accident, little girls from St. Vincent's were skipping across the Franklin Street Bridge to get to St. Anthony's Grade School. This was the same bridge that crossed the railroad tracks.

There must have been half a dozen other ways to travel back and forth, always hitting our favorite spots in the neighborhood: the Redemptorist House where Father Adler lived, Catholic University, College Pharmacy, Safeway and the Newman Catholic Bookstore. It was a fascinating neighborhood.

The B&O Railroad tracks were supposed to be closed off to pedestrians. You could travel under the Franklin Street Bridge as well as over it to get to school. Without a chain link fence, barbed wire or mad barking dogs to keep you out, the railroad tracks beckoned you to come play.

"Climb over my tracks—you will get to school faster! Throw rocks and pennies on me to see if an oncoming train can flatten them. Walk my railroad ties in time to your internal musical clock. Lie face down on my tracks when a train is coming to prove you've got guts!"

I succumbed to the lure of the train whistle lots of times, when all was quiet on the tracks, skipping over each wooden railroad tie, arms outstretched for balance, singing my favorite song, "Never Smile at a Crocodile" at the top of my lungs, jumping on to the next wooden tie with each syllable of my song. Yet, I could barely imagine walking over the tracks facing an oncoming train without panicking.

Lying face down on the tracks was a challenge. Lots of kids did it effortlessly. There was actually enough room on the tracks to lie face down without injury from the passing train. In the sixth grade, with an ever-growing, rounded fanny, I was warned that my rump was going to be scraped off and carried to Chicago with the train. I practiced lying down like Penelope Pitstop many times while there were no trains in sight, but I never had the guts, for this and so many other fun childhood games, to GO ALL THE WAY!

I liked St. Anthony's more than St. Pete's, especially since we didn't have to travel so long to get there. I had a great bunch of girlfriends and we chummed around together a little before and after school when I could justify leaving St. Vincent's early or leaving school late to go back home. Sometimes I said we might be having a special Mass at church and Sister at St. Vincent's would say to go half an hour early just in case we did. Staying longer after school did not require a fib. There were lots of reasons to be late, anything from helping count the number of subscriptions sold in the fifth grade or doling out the prizes for *The Catholic Standard* to helping Sister Ann Louis wash blackboards.

The after-school gatherings were mostly passing around gossip with my best friend at school, Kathleen Croake, about fellow classmates, and even world politics, at least the politics that could interest a fifth grader in the 1950s. It was the year when Elvis Presley, *King of Rock and Roll*, was drafted into the Army. One girl's brother, who was in his platoon, wrote her letters and always included a little information about Elvis. We even saw a real photograph of him sitting on his bunk.

Elvis had just been assigned to Company "D," 1st Battalion, 32nd Armory, 3rd Armored Division of the 7th Army, in Friedberg, West Germany. We thought that this was an important job. Years later we found out he did nothing more than drive a Lt. Col. around in a jeep. But we respected him because "he did his time."

Our sixth grade teacher, Mrs. Higgins, was a lay teacher who lived across the street from school. She embarrassed me one time. We had a school bake sale and there was one cupcake left at the end of the day. Mrs. Higgins announced that she was giving it to me because

"Juanita lives at the home and they don't have their mothers there to bake them after-school snacks." Everyone looked at me with pity. It was sickening! I threw the cupcake in the trash can.

Paula Bryant, a seventh grader at St. Anthony's, was a very special friend who also lived at St. Vincent's. Her teacher took a special interest in her and invited her to stay at her home on weekends and holidays. Paula fit in very well with her teacher's family and was eventually adopted by them. The Bryant family must have had some luck going for them because one of the other girls was also adopted by a marvelous family in Western Maryland. Their older sister was a nun. I was very envious.

God, at Home and at School

1. Who made us?
God made us.
2. Who is God?
God is the Supreme Being, infinitely perfect, who made all
things and keeps them in existence.
3. Why did God make us?
God made us to show forth His goodness and to share with us
His everlasting happiness in heaven.
4. What must we do to gain the happiness of heaven?
To gain the happiness of heaven we must know, love, and serve
God in this world.

The Baltimore Catechism, together with a number of special
booklets, a "pre-Catechism" in the early grades, designed to assist the
second-grader making his or her First Holy Communion, individual
books on the lives of the saints, and the Holy Bible, Catholic school
students were equipped with the necessary literature about the
Catholic faith and had the formula for following the word of God and
gaining "the happiness of heaven."

The No. 2 Saint Joseph Baltimore Catechism contained all of the
answers to all of the great mysteries in a child's life. It was written
with "for the middle and upper grades of grammar school" and
included hundreds of drawings. Explanations and pictures were

used profusely to help the children understand each lesson.

Every basic topic of the faith was covered in simple straightforward language: Prayers for Every day-13 prayers, beginning with the Sign of the Cross through the Prayers before and after meals; Part One: The Creed; Part Two: The Commandments; Part Three: The Sacraments and Prayer. The Catechism also included photographs of the Holy Land and the Mass, with the responses for the Priest and the people.

One of the great features of the use of the Baltimore Catechism in Catholic schools was that it was universal—the same text was used in the thousands of schools throughout the country. Children were expected to memorize everything in the Catechism.

Second grade was probably the most eventful year at school for me. This is when I received the sacraments of Penance and Holy Communion. Second grade is also when Catholic school children learn "cursive." My cousin Janice told me that at Brent School where she attended you just fell into handwriting a year or two after you learned to print. You did not have "Penmanship" as an actual subject in the public school. Sister showed us on the blackboard how to set up your notebook paper every day before you wrote anything.

You drew a cross in the center at the very top of the page. You had this reminder of Jesus hanging on the cross for you. Under this you wrote "J.M.J." You dedicated your work to "Jesus, Mary and Joseph." Sometimes Sister might give you extra credit on a quiz for remembering to put the cross and J.M.J. at the top of your paper. She almost always took off points if you forgot it.

Janice never mentioned children in her school being slapped or hit or cracked with a ruler. We heard stories about children "in the olden days" being beaten for having poor penmanship. Luckily it never happened at St. Peter's but I do remember Sister being a little stricter with the boys, mostly because the boys misbehaved more than the girls. We also had several boys who developed really big ears. They were chronically yanked by Sister when they needed to be pulled from a situation quickly and forcibly.

In an era before my days at St. Vincent's, Sister Lucia or Sister Helen would awaken the girls with a single clap of the hands and a prayer.

"Good Morning, Sweet Jesus, My Savior.
Good Morning, Sweet Mary, My Mother.
Keep Me from Sin this Day and Always."

By that time the girls were in their robes, kneeling by the foot of their beds. Time to rise and shine. Many more prayers followed.

At St. Vincent's the Angelus bell rang at six o'clock every evening. We had heard the prayer many times at school and at home: "The Angel of the Lord declared declared unto Mary...and she conceived of the Holy Spirit...Pray for us Holy Mother of God, that we may become worthy of the promises of Christ..." The ringing of the bell was a reminder for reflection.

We believed in angels—good and bad angels. And we believed we were each given a personal "guardian angel" who guided and took care of us. When we saw people downtown talking to themselves we laughed and assumed that they were just "having a conversation with their guardian angel."

The added protection was no insurance policy for playing fearlessly in the Grove or diving off the side of swimming pool into shallow water. Admittedly, sometimes we used the fact that we had a guardian angel as a pretext for behaving irresponsibly.

Vatican II opened on October 11, 1962 with the greatest representation of priests ever held in an assembly—2,500. In his opening remarks, Pope John XXIII declared that the purpose of Vatican II was a "pastoral" council which was concerned with representing the Catholic faith in a manner acceptable to the modern world.

What came out of Vatican II were marked changes in the Liturgy that were studied and debated for years. There were changes in practical ways that affected your everday life as an American Catholic. In the late 1960s a consortium of Catholic universities declared that their schools would be free from any external governance, including Rome's ecclesiastical oversight. More liberal, "problematic" catechisms appeared. The sexual revolution of the 1960s and the overall moral decline of the times resulted in a great deal of dissent from the Church's teachings on contraception, divorce, marriage and co-habitation.

Without engaging in any of these activities at the tender age of 18, the change that had the most influence on me was the use of the vernacular language in lieu of Latin for the Mass. Even though I did not study Latin in high school, for me the language held a great mystique and charm unlike saying prayers in English. Initially, the Mass in English somehow seemed less reverent.

We were encouraged to attend daily Mass at St. Vincent's. This required getting up at 6:00 instead of 6:30 a.m. to get ready. On Sundays we got up at 7:00 for a 7:30 a.m. Mass. You fasted from midnight until after Mass without even a drop of water. Failing to adhere to the fast was a reason for not receiving Communion. You also had to be in the "state of grace." Several times a girl would tell Sister, "I brushed my teeth by mistake" and she was not able to receive Communion; the true reason was that she had not confessed a "mortal" sin in Confession or her conscience bothered her about something in some other way.

There were no altar boys and a high school girl or one of the Sisters would respond to the prayers of the Mass. At the Communion rail, Father handed the paten to the first person receiving Communion and she passed it to the next person.

Before going to confession at school, Sister would set aside a few minutes for an "Examination of Conscience," heads down on the desk with your eyes closed for concentration. It was a time to reflect on what transgressions had occurred since your last confession. You would categorize your sins into "mortal"—serious sins that keep you away from the grace of God or "venial"—less grevious offenses.

In the upper grades there were clever little cards that would list the areas of wrongdoing. It certainly made telling on yourself a lot easier. Organization was good also because it made your confession less confusing to the priest. If the priest had to prod and pull the information out of you because you were so disorganized, he was likely to figuratively throw the book at you and give you a huge penance.

On the first Friday of each month we attended Mass at our individual school churches. Afterwards we would pile out of church and into the school cafeteria to break our fast with a "Breakfast of

Champions" that consisted of a handful of Krispy Kreme glazed donuts and a bottle of Tru-Ade orange soda.

Every Friday afternoon at St. Vincent's, Father Adler gave Benediction, a traditional ceremony was for the purpose of exposition of the consecrated Host in the "monstrance." Father would bless us in the form of the cross with the monstrance, the beautiful gold-laden vessel, while incense was disbursed and a small bell was rung. Then the Host was reposed in the Tabernacle. The familiar Latin hymns were sung: "Tantum Ergo" and "O Salutaris." Father concluded with the "Divine Praises," a litany of prayers in English, "Blessed be God, blessed be His holy name...."

"Bring Flowers of the fairest, bring flowers of the rarest, from garden and woodland and hillside and vale. Our full hearts are swelling, our glad voices telling, the praise of the loveliest rose of the dale..."

May Processions can be quite elaborate in parish churches. We were permitted to participate in our May Procession in our school's church. The tradition at St. Peter's was to walk from the Church around a park just a few blocks away, singing hymns to Mary the Mother of Jesus whose special month was the month of May. Several boys carried a crowned statue of the Blessed Mother mounted on a platform, toted on two long poles. The Rosary was said as we marched in procession, each grade walking together to form the huge long line of students from Kindergarten through the eighth grade. When we returned to the Church the "May Queen,"—an eighth grader who had been selected to serve, carried fresh cut flowers and crowned the Blessed Mother statue with a of fresh flowers.

"O Mary we crown thee with blossoms today. Queen of the Angels, Queen of the May. O Mary we crown thee with blossoms today. Queen of the Angels, Queen of the May."

At St. Vincent's the May Procession lead from the front hallway, completely around the grounds of St. Vincent's then back to the building and into the chapel for Benediction. Occasionally, several altar boys from St. Joseph's Home would be present to assist Father Adler. There were three statues of the Blessed Mother outdoors—one in the front of the grounds, one to the side and one in the Grove. All three statues were crowned and a different May Queen was selected for each coronation; the final crowning was held in the chapel.

The chapel was right down the hall from us. It felt as though God were truly with us. The buildings and the grounds had religious statues and pictures that reminded us constantly that we were protected and held in the bosom of Our Lord. We always considered ourselves to be especially protected and harbored from all injury. Our home was truly our Sanctuary.

Putting on a Show

T'was the wearing of the green, the speaking with a brogue, and a curtain about to rise when Sister Mary Frances was around. Everyone was an "honorary "colleen" — an Irish girl, not just on St. Patrick's Day but throughout the year. A petite little woman with thick glasses that sat on her thin nose, Sister Mary Frances' spirit was very much like one of her favorite songs:

"Sure a little bit of heaven fell from out the sky one day, and it nestled in the ocean in a spot so far away....and when the angels found it sure it looked so peaceful there.....so they sprinkled it with stardust just to make the shamrocks grow. 'Tis the only place you'll find them no matter where you go...and when they had it finished sure they called it Ireland."

Her productions for St. Patrick's Day were galas. St. Vincent's was blessed with many talented singers and entertainers, and she showed them off every year. Melody Simms, Alicia and Cora Panganiban, Amelia Peña, Barbara Loveless, Mary Elizabeth Lyons.

The sets resembled professionally-made structures. There were real picket fences covered in real flowers, wooden benches and backdrops that gave an authentic Irish cottage woodsy feel to the scene. And the costumes, although painstakingly sewn by several of the Sisters, could rival the professional wardrobes from Broadway shows.

Sister Mary Frances was in command of every single detail, from the music to the costumes and the scenery, to the programs and the audience. While she knew how rare it is to have that caliber of musical talent available to her, she had a little less respect for the art of dance and felt that anyone could learn to do the Irish jig. As a matter of fact, she did the choreography herself and taught us the dances. She would hike up her heavy wool habit, displaying her skinny little legs in dark stockings and her agile little feet in the heavy clodhopper-type heels, in order to have you follow her dance steps, most of which she made up on the spot.

Hope Baza had quite a difficult time when she learned to tap dance from Sister Mary Frances. Sister had to place her on the left side of the stage so she wouldn't bump into everyone else in the show, even though Hope would eventually end up off the stage and behind the curtains.

Sister accepted no excuses for not participating in the show. The group sisters would back her up too. No nonsense. She simply assigned you a part and you performed! Sister Mary Frances was a professional. Sometimes you played the role of a boy, now matter how much you protested, even though you had long hair. This could easily be disguised. Besides believing that anyone could dance, she said many times, especially when one of the Filipinas tried to get out of being in the play because of nationality, "Everyone is a little bit Irish. Sure and begorra!"

Sister's shows did not stop at St. Patrick's Day. She had Christmas pageants for which we rehearsed for hours to get the hymns just right. And there were plays and other musical programs through the year.

A Christmas show we put on ended with the song made popular by Perry Como. I can never recall the opening words, even when Sister Mary Frances spent hours rehearsing with us. The words spell out the word Christmas.

"C is for the Christ child, born on Christmas Day,
H for herald angels in the night,
R for our Redeemer,
I means Israel, and
S is for the star that shone so bright.

T is for three wisemen, they who traveled far,
M is for the manger where He laid,
A's for all He stands for,
S means shepherds came.
And that's why there's a Christmas Day."

Another year Sister Mary Frances taught us a beautiful song for a show which we performed on Mother's Day.

"M is for the million things she gave me.
O means only that she's growing old.
T is for the tears she shed to save me.
H is for her heart of purest gold.
E for eyes with love light shining.
R for right, and right she'll always be.
Put them all together they spell MOTHER,
The word that means the world to me."

Mom did not come for the show. No phone calls. No explanations. She showed up weeks later, decked out in a low-cut silk dress and red high heels, with a shopping bag full of candy and nuts. Her flaming red hair was thick and bushy and swept up on her head in a French twist. The other girls said she was the sexiest mom they had ever seen.

We shared all of the candy with them, even our favorites — the dark chocolate non-pareils, pistachios and cashews. Sister, apparently did not want the likes of a woman like Christine Helphenstine Mondoñedo around the St. Vincent girls. She let MM and I walk her back to the streetcar stop on Rhode Island Avenue. Something held us back from jumping on the streetcar with her. We left a trail of pistachio shells from the car stop to St. Vincent's fantasizing that she'd follow the shells back to us and take us home for good.

We had an opportunity to sing the "MOTHER" song at my godmother's house. My *Ninang* Maria, and *Ninong* Joseph Castillion invited us over for dinner to their apartment which was across the street from the Old Pension Building on Fourth Street. To us they were *Ninang Maria* or *Ninong José*, or simply "Mary" and "Joe." I was the eldest of her 20 godchildren, and she told me often that I was her most special godchild. Many of her godchildren lived in this same huge apartment building, including a godson who had been born a "blue baby" at Columbia Hospital. She explained it had something to do with his breathing. We still could not understand how he changed colors. He looked as tan to us as any of the other Mexicans and Filipinos in the building

Mary cried when MM and I performed the "MOTHER" song for her guests. She wanted so much for our family to be reunited and would invite Mom and Dad at the same time, just to see if they could be in the same room and talk like civilized beings.

Nothing seemed to work and Dad continued to pine for her for years. She never had anything good to say about him. Dad always made excuses for Mom's behavior. She had done so much to destroy his life yet he never uttered a bad word against her when we were around.

MM and I thought sometimes that it was a never-ending movie. It was like watching two characters on a stage, acting out their pitiful lives in front of a camera. We always wished that we could have re-written the script. It certainly would have had a much happier ending.

Keeping Christ in Christmas

Easter Sunday was the attestation that Christ, by His resurrection from the dead, was indeed the Lord and Savior. But without a doubt, the Christmas season at St. Vincent's was the highlight of the year for most of us.

From Ash Wednesday, the start of "Advent," we were strongly encouraged to attend Mass on a daily basis if we were not already in the habit of doing so every morning. Midnight Mass at St. Vincent's was held in the evening but not necessarily at midnight. Before Midnight Mass, the "big" girls' choir from the older groups came to the "little" girls groups and sang Christmas carols. Then everyone went into the chapel for Midnight Mass.

The chapel was decorated with pot after pot of bright fresh velvety poinsettia plants, clustered together and interspersed with garlands of pine branches and pine cones. Traditionally placed at the right side of the altar, the Nativity creche surrounded by fresh cut pine trees, took up the entire space. The statues, painted so realistically, were at least four feet high; the stable was almost life-sized. The Christ Child was left out of the scene until Midnight Mass, then He appeared lying in the manger amidst the straw, His family and the stable animals.

Almost everyone went home for a few days during the holidays. If you had no family you might go home with another girl and her family. And there were always volunteers who wanted to take one or two girls home with them to their homes for the holidays. It was a time to be spoiled by adults. We felt the kindness of strangers in so many ways.

Anderson Jewelers near the corner of 11th and G Streets would accept old watches from the public. They would fix them up and donate them to charities at Christmas time, St. Vincent's being one of the receiving homes of the watches.

If we wrote out Christmas cards to friends or family, we would never think of writing "Xmas," using the X for the word "Christ." It was just not keeping "Christ" in Christmas. The decorations we put up in our classrooms at school were festive but they paled by comparison to the decorations we put up around our home, around St. Vincent's during the holidays. Each group, of course had its own Christmas tree, usually a tree eight feet tall or higher, with ornaments and tinsel to generously fill each branch.

Outside, a live Christmas tree was placed atop the porch that was over the portico of the main entrance. It was usually covered with bright, colorful lights and the five-pointed star placed on the building above the tree could be seen all the way from Union Station.

There was no ugly competition going on. Each group seemed to have something unique placed on the walls or tables of their living quarters. One year in Group One we had a three-foot high Advent calendar. As each day ended we would lift the cardboard tab with the date to find out a new activity that we could do. The activities were acts of kindness like turning down someone's bed for them in the evening or bringing their dishes to the kitchen sink or the cart after meals.

Everyone had an Advent wreath which sat on a table somewhere in each dining room. It was lit every night during dinner. The Advent wreath was made of evergreen and had three purple candles to remind us to do penance and one pink candle to remind us that Christmas was very near.

In Sister Bernard's group we put our names in a bowl and each girl would chose a *Kriskan,* a Christ Child. The name you had chosen was to be kept secret. You could do little favors for your *Kriskan* throughout the Advent season. Finishing her "duty" for her. Giving your Kriskan your dessert when she wasn't looking.

Before my era at St. Vincent's, opening Christmas presents was celebrated on Christmas morning. But so many girls went home for the holidays so on "Little Christmas"—January 6th—Epiphany—we received our Christmas presents. It seemed very appropriate since this day commemorated the coming of the Magi to Bethlehem; the three wisemen bore gifts for the newborn Christchild.

The Ladies Auxiliary with the invaluable manpower of Rita McAuliff, Katharine Nally, Marie and Selma Frank and many others was the backbone behind the elfin magic that occurred magically each year. Each girl could ask for things, from the youngest to the oldest; their wishes were written down. There were donations of toys. But for most of the shopping, the Sisters would shop downtown—Hecht's, Woodies, Lansburgh's, Kann's.

Then sorting and wrapping, the volunteers worked in the locked "Santa Claus Room" which was in the basement. The large "play room" in each group was locked. Some years huge Christmas trees would be set up with large platforms around them. These were decorated with snow scenes and such by Ellen Glynn and others who did not believe in Santa Claus. Ellen knew that the "believers" were certain Santa Claus did everything.

Each girl was given a jam-packed array of Christmas presents. Coats, umbrellas, boots, underwear, skirts, blouses, jewelry, jewelry boxes, hair curlers, toiletries. Multitudes of presents for each girl were chosen, customized by size, favorite colors and specific taste. The presents differed from year to year.

Each year one special garment was always included—a petticoat—a cotton slip. A slip was synonymous with Christmas, and as you matured the slips, either "full" or "half" slips, were a true present of luxury, for they were made of nylon or silk or some other lustrous material.

From the beginning of Advent until the Feast of the Epiphany the whole season felt like nylon or silk! Filled with anticipation, just like magic, it was silky, velvety, rich. While this season was overflowing with the receipt of many material goods we knew the true meaning of Christmas—the celebration of the birth of Christ. We relived it each year through every word of every hymn, every picture from every Christmas card, every twinkle from every light, every jingle from every bell. Christ was born for us in Bethlehem.

We Were Only Human

We did a good job of telling our sins to Father Adler in confession. But many times a sin might not exactly fit the "mortal sin" or "venial sin" categories. And some of the "naughty" things you hid were not necessarily sins. Some of the lies you told as children, the "little white lies," also might not have qualified as sins to be confessed. Frankly, we were only human, and some of our shenanigans were never revealed.

During Catherine DeForge's time in the days when you attended school right at home at St. Vincent's, you were not allowed to bring books into the dormitories. So in the middle of the night when Sister turned the lights out, the girls would congregate in the lavatories, each one sitting on the toilet in her own locked stall. If there were a noise and Sister had to investigate, she checked under the partitions. Seeing no feet on the ground she went back to her cell. The girls who had lifted their feet so they wouldn't be detected, would then lower their feet and breath a little easier.

Eva and Anna Neidringhaus slept in the two beds in the alcove near the statue of St. Joseph. Once in bed at night, you were not allowed get up to go to the lavatory for a drink. The bottle of holy water that Sister sprinkled on all of the girls at bedtime was kept in the stand beneath the statue. So when Eva and Anna were thirsty they drank from the holy water and filled up the bottle every day with unblessed water.

Often when it was still light outside and the girls had been put to bed, Eva and Anna waited until Sister's recreation and night prayers were over when she would come to her cell for bed. As soon as her light went out, they raided the broom closets for mops and brooms to have play battles.

Sister hearing the ruckus called out, "What is happening?"

"There's just a bat or two loose," they replied. Sister's light would go out quickly and the "highjinks" would continue on for a while. No one ever expected to see Sister without her habit, but once a substitute was in the cell when the imaginary bat came. This Daughter of Charity was concerned about the girls' safety and she came out of the cell without her cornette! They were caught. But the shock from seeing Sister without the cornette was even more scandalous.

Information was POWER! M.Y.O.B. This was a very popular saying at the time. It meant Mind Your Own Business! We did a lot of sneaking around to find out things that were not really our business. One thing that was so important was finding out Sister's "family name." We were not privy to this information until after Vatican II. Being assigned to work in the Sister's Refectory and sneaking into their "Community Room" was the best way of learning that important fact. Knowledge was power even back then.

Sneaking around in the Sister's Community Room was also a great way to catch them in the act of EATING. This very human act—eating in front of the girls—is something that was banned in those days.

Sister Loretta hid candy bars on the top edges of open doors as a way of checking whether the edges got dusted. She knew how to get a job done!

One of the nuns left some candy in a small box. Some of the girls found the candy and ate it. The next day there was a note pinned to the wall that said, "Thou shalt not steal." One wise girl wrote her own note, "Thou shalt not lead us into temptation!"

We had nicknames for each of the nuns, many of which will go to our graves unrevealed. In Mary Pauline Perello's freshman year there was a Sister named Sister Mary John. The girls called her "Sister Johnny" behind her back. One day Sister Serena and Sister Mary John were in the high school dorm. This was before intercoms, extension lines, pagers and cell phones. Mary Pauline was told to tell Sister

Mary John that she had a very important telephone message. She ran to the dorm, got Sister Serena's attention and said, "Sister Johnny has an important telephone call." Sister Serena made her repeat herself three times before Mary Pauline realized what she said. No punishment was given but Mary Pauline was certainly embarrassed.

Girls were frequently dispatched from the office to run around the huge building to deliver messages in this way. In most instances, when you were on "official business" dictated from the office, you were given permission to save time from running up the steps by using the small elevator that went from the third floor to the basement. When no one was watching your every move, however, you might decide to ride "Otis" just for the fun of it!

Regina Mooney and several other girls were asked to serve refreshments to Archbishop O'Boyle. It was 1958. The girls did not know that it was a Board of Directors meeting of Catholic Charities being held at St. Vincent's. The girls flipped a coin and Regina got to serve the Archbishop. She could hear the cup shaking in the saucer in one hand, the coffee pot in the other, as she stood behind the Archbishop. Afraid that Regina would pour the coffee on his head, he turned around and held the cup for her.

Later the girls served the dessert—huge chunks of strawberry shortcake with gobs of real whipped cream. Serving the Archbishop from the right as she had been instructed, she tried to be do well. He looked up at her and said, "Missy, you take this dessert for yourself. I had better stay on my diet." Regina went back to the kitchen with a huge smile on her face and started eating away.

The girls of St. Vincent's were blessed to have reminders and symbols both at home and at school that God loved us. At school the Sisters would give us holy cards when we had excelled on a test or had done something equally noteworthy. At home the Sisters would do the same for some special act of kindness we might have performed around the group.

By the time I was in the sixth grade I had accumulated about 30 or 40 holy cards. I used them as bookmarks but they would constantly fall out of my Sunday Missal or my New Testament. The boys at St. Anthony's would collect baseball and football cards and I knew that my collection of holy cards was getting as large as any of their sports collections. One day at lunchtime out on the playground a boy named Billy, whose mother worked at the rectory, grabbed my cards and said we should play *FISH* with them. We knew this was sacreligious and might even constitute a mortal sin. Maybe this was cause for burning in hell! But before we knew it he was dealing us each a hand and we were playing *Fish*. Who could resist a game of cards

"Give me all of your "St. Patricks." (The cards did not have to match exactly, they just had to be of the same type.)

"FISH!"

"Okay then, give me all of your "Our Lady of Perpetual Helps."

"FISH!"

Most of my holy cards were just one of a kind from nuns who were one of a kind. Not many pairs. My matching game didn't last very long. I never disclosed to the Sisters at home that we played this game at school.

There was a Sister at St. Vincent's whose profile was so much like that of Pope Pius XII, it was almost frightening. She was a dead ringer for the Pope. The rumor going around the groups was that they were brother and sister. We knew it couldn't be true because the Holy Father was Italian and the Sister was from Boston. But it got a lot of attention anyway.

Later in my high school days, I was guilty of a silly shenanigan related to the Holy Father. I was on the honor roll at St. Patrick's but came home with an "F" on a history quiz. Sister at school was shocked at my grade and told me to have Sister at home sign the quiz. I remembered a story Dad told me about when he enlisted in the Navy in the Philippines. The recruiter asked the 16-year-old "Pinoy" in front of Dad in line for his birth certificate. The young Filipino said, "The records from my town were destroyed when the church was burned." The excuse worked, so Dad used the same line and it worked for him. I thought a variation of the story would work for me too.

I went to the open incinerator outside of the main kitchen and tossed my quiz into the shooting flames. I knew that one quiz would not hurt my final grade. No embarrassment. No hassle. I stayed by the incinerator until the paper turned to ashes. Making the sign of the cross over the flames I said, "Remember man that thou art dust and unto dust thou shalt return."

Then, excited about my little game, I got more brazen. Raising my head to Heaven with both hands in the air, I turned on my best Italian accent and shouted, "We got-a white smoke-a. Praise-a be to God. We got-a new Pope-a!" One of the cooks walked by just as I was making a sacriligeous fool of myself but she ignored me and I went back to Sister Bernard's group, feeling just a little guilty.

Gone for the Weekend

We didn't spend much time at Aunt Edna's house on the weekends because Dad still had his responsibilities for serving meals to his boss in Northwest. Aunt Edna lived beyond Southeast in Oxon Run Hills, Maryland, so if we were only permitted to spend the day with our family, Dad would pick us up after he served lunch and had to bring us back to St. Vincent's before 7:00 p.m. Ocassionally we brought along a friend or two from St. Vincent's, someone who was not going home with their family.

When we were permitted to spend the weekend, we usually stayed at Dad's boss' home in Northwest also. Dad had a reputation among the girls of St. Vincent's for being an excellent cook. He had a rule about after-dinner desserts: You had to spell our last name: MONDONEDO. Then you would get your dessert. All of the girls that came home with us thought that it was worth every letter and every syllable!

MM and I were rarely bored. Dad bought us a little Philco television set and we would watch cartoons or variety shows all day, something we could not do at St. Vincent's. If Dad had to work in his taxicab for a few hours, we entertained ourselves in the gliders on the front porch of Major Wills' home. We stole marzipan and Avignone Freres-baked goodies from Major's kitchen and had festive tea parties alfresco.

There were two ladies that lived on third floor of Major Wills' house that provided a lot of fascination for us when we would visit Dad where he lived and worked. We fantasized that they were part of a harem that Major kept at his home. The truth is they were both sixtyish, school-teacher types who proved to be accomplished, intelligent women who happened to be renting rooms from Major Wills. The heat from any potential sexual escapades was simmering in our over-active, adolescent imaginations only.

One Christmas Eve we walked in the snow from Ashmead Place to Columbia Road and found that they were giving away fresh scotch pine Christmas trees to anyone who could carry one home. We begged Dad to drag one home, which he finally consented to do—a distance of about a mile. We had no Christmas ornaments but Dad had some spray snow which we used liberally to decorate the tree. We made a star out of aluminum foil, strings of seashell macaroni and stood back, admiring our homemade wonder. This was a lot of fun. Making ornaments for the tree didn't seem as "down-home" and backward as some of Dad's other do-it-yourself activities.

Dad would make his own shoe polish for patent leather shoes—he'd rub the shiny surface with the inside skin of a banana peel, telling us this was how they did it in the Philippines when he was a kid. We suspected that when he was a kid at the turn of the 19th century, patent leather had not been yet been invented and definitely not brought to the Philippine Islands by the Spanish or the Americans. But we could not be sure.

Another homemade idea, one equally embarrassing if it were made known to our peers, was his homemade coconut grater—a 6" x 18" flat piece of wood attached to a crude scraping tool and nailed into the plywood. He would straddle the plywood with the scraper-gadget between his legs, a large bowl directly under it, and whittle away at the fresh, juicy coconut meat. We thought he went to extreme lengths for something that would be consumed in 10 minutes or less, but it made a lot more than you would get in a dried-up bag of grated Baker's coconut from the grocery store.

If we did not have a Christmas gift for the Rillons, we would go shopping with Dad on Christmas Eve and take advantage of the great bargains. They wanted to get the Christmas stock sold, so almost everything at Dart Drug or People's was half the original price. We felt we could justify buying twice as much.

Ocassionally we spent a night or the whole weekend at Aunt Edna's. Her neighborhood was not as intriguing as the old neighborhood at Capitol Hill. If it weren't for the People's Drug Store with the soda fountain and the High's Dairy Store with the five cents per scoop ice cream cones, we would have had nothing to do.

Dad frequented the M&B Restaurant in Chinatown, named for the Filipinos who owned it. He also attended the dances at the Willard, the USO, and what he referred to as the "dime-a-dance clubs." Somewhere in this social arena, through mutual friends, our Uncle Joe and our Aunt Grace, he met my mother, Christine Helphenstine Simms, AKA "Teenie." He was born in 1897. She was born in 1926. Whenever he told us the story of their first meeting, he dramatized it just a little bit.

"From across the room I saw such a gorgeous young American lady and immediately fell in love. Her red hair shining in the evening, her satin gown twinkling just for me, she beckoned me, flashing her deep, dark brown eyes and pursing her pouty, ruby red lips—c'mon, Sailor Boy, dance with me...it's your dime!"

The dances were sponsored by Filipino social clubs—the Vicente Lim Post V.F.W. or the Benevolent Brotherhood of the Visayas, or some such titles. The longer the name, the more impressive. I am not certain who they were trying to impress. They were open to any and all Filipinos, whether you were born *blue seal*, on this side of the Pacific, just like the blue seal on cigarettes, or lovingly pronounced with "P" for "F" and vice versa, *fure bludded Pilipinos*. There was one club for a fellow countryman, *kababayan*, of Ilocos, but of course everyone spoke Tagalog and English. One club boasted "for professionals only."

The people that were in charge of these clubs had names like *Asunción, Corazón, Concepción, Natividad,* even *Perpetua* and *Imaculata*. Reading them off the list of the "sponsors" or folks to whom kudos were given, it sounded like the litany of the saints, or a list of movable-calendar church feast days, not in Latin but in Filipinized Spanish.

Filipinos love to give speeches. They love using words like "gregarious," "provocative" or "indigenous," and other words that contain twice as many syllables to showoff an educated command of the English language. By the time the usual *maraming salamat* sentiments were passed out, everyone in the entire ballroom had been thanked, even before the dance had started. There were many reasons for thanking everyone.They had helped put the dance together. They were related to someone who helped. They drove with someone who helped. Or they were from the same town in the Philippines as someone who helped, and on and on and on. Each of these individuals was acknowledged at least once before the dance could commence.

First and second generation Filipinos, professionals and non-professionals—linked together socially. What connected them all was their interest in the Philippines and the music. Primarily it was the music that compelled you to dress up—anything from a tuxedo and long gown to cocktail clothing was appropriate—and to spend a small fortune on the entrance to the dance and parking at the hotel. And during the dance, there were raffles and 50-50 chances and more speeches to boast about the wonderful charitable works the association was providing. The hotel that was chosen was usually the Willard, downtown on 15th Street. But we ocassionaly went to the Sheraton-Park Hotel or the Hotel Harrington.

The Saturday night dances, geared to a more adult patronage but still permitting a few children, were wonderful. The D.C. area Filipinos loved the rhumba, the tango, the cha-cha-cha and any other form of ballroom dancing that showed you and your partner off. One band in particular, The Caballeros, had a wonderful variety of music—from a five-minute rendition of "Cherry Pink and Apple Blossom White" that proudly showed off their talented trumpet player, or to simpler tunes, like "The Bunny Hop" or the "Conga"—anything that would get the masses dancing and having a wonderful time. They would wear Hawaiian shirts and leis one week, and tuxedos the next, according to their whim.

There were just a handful of old biddies off in the corner gossiping about who was out with whom. But almost everyone was on the dance floor all night. You felt comfortable dancing male with female, female with female, and or just on the floor by yourself! And after the cash bar had operated a few hours, even the old biddies were on the floor, tapping the women on their shoulders to cut in on their partners. Just before one o'clock the band would always play

"Goodnight Ladies" and everyone would depart from the hotel. But it was not over, for half the patrons showed up at the various restaurants in Chinatown for a midnight meal.

Luscious succulent pork lo mein, tender beef with *ampalaya*—bittermelon—and garlic-soaked shrimp with lobster sauce always taste best at two in the morning. The variety of dishes was endless, just like the different dialects and languages being spoken around the tables of the restaurants.

While you were waiting for your dinner, the *sikoy-sikoy* man would come around. This may be a made-up Tagalog name for the Chinese man who let you "mark your spot" on his lottery sheets. For 71 cents you could choose 7 spots and take your chances that these would be the lucky winning spots for the evening. The sheets had about 100 Chinese characters spread out on the thin white paper. You just used his marker to color in the characters. We rarely played the game that gave you twice as many spots—it cost $1.42.

"You win more money for less money," Dad said. The Chinese man would mark the spots you had chosen on his sheet, give you a copy, collect your money and be gone in a flash, before the cops knew what was happening. Dad said there were lots of raids on the operation. The "office" was just the back room of a laundry in a private home on H Street.

The timing was good. By the time you finished your meal, the *sikoy-sikoy* man would be back with the results of the lottery. The winning characters were punched out with a hole puncher on his sheet. He would just lay the "answer sheet" over your sheet and pay you cash immediately if you had four or more of the same spots marked. Many times we won about $20 and used it for the meal.

At three o'clock, a man would come around selling *The Washington Post*. Armed with your newspaper you could finally end the day and go home to bed. When we were little girls living at St. Vincent's, we viewed the dances as a wonderful departure from the usual 9:00 o'clock bedtime we adhered to normally. When we returned to St. Vincent's these adventures provided lots of fodder for stories to tell the other girls at St. Vincent's.

Summertime Livin' Was Easy

Melody Simms created the mood when she sang the little girls a lullaby to get us to sleep on hot summer nights—it was the famous song with the dreamy words from "Porgy and Bess (Summertime)." Other favorites were the songs made popular by Frankie Laine— "Ghost Riders in the Sky" and "Mule Train."

Melody would stare off into space, hands and arms circling in the air, as though she were a voodoo dancer in a trance, singing the words "yippee yi ay" in *Ghost Riders* and she would yell, making the cracking whip sounds by snapping her leather belt on the iron bars of one of the beds for the song "Mule Train." It was better than the movies.

The living was easy at St. Vincent's in the summertime. While everyone else in the city sweltered from the heat and humidity, we lived the "Life of Riley." We had a wonderful back yard with swings and picnic tables. But the greatest luxury was the pool. It was 70 feet by 45 feet, with a wading area at one end for the little ones and a deeper area with a diving board at the other end. It was cool and refreshing. And with the exception of waiting 30 minutes after a light meal or an hour after a heavy meal, for our health's sake to "avoid getting cramps," we were always in the pool.

The pool was originally built in 1933, through the labor of Mr. William Carrigan, a seminarian from Catholic University, who, with the aid of friends determined, "The prayers of the little children should not go unanswered any longer."

They started digging a hole for the pool, a very labor-intensive project. They began by hitching up a plow and horse from the seminary. Realizing this would take months to do, they solicited help from the owner of a bulldozer and managed to reduce the cost of the pool from $7,000 to under $1,500.

You had to wear a bathing cap in the pool for sanitary reasons, we were told. The caps smashed your hair and made you look stupid. But they kind of served as a helmet when you dove into the pool off the diving board. Most of the girls prided themselves for their appearance; no one wanted to look like an orphan, of course. The drab bathing caps did not help.

Every photograph taken in those days emphasized the dowdy look of an orphan because of the bathing cap. Some of the girls had such big ears they showed through the cap making it look like an aviator cap, especially if you wore a pair of snorkeling goggles. To look cool, you unsnapped the band that went under your chin, hooking it up behind your head, letting your ponytail hang down in the back.

Some of the older girls helped us pass the Red Cross exam for swimming, timing us as we treaded water in the deep area of the pool. In order to pass the next level and get the Red Cross certificate you had to jump into the water with your clothes on, tread water a few minutes, remove your clothes, and hold on to them while swimming to the edge of the pool.

Our designated instructors could be cruel. They even made us untie our shoes before removing them, a task that is almost impossible when you are immersed in water. They also seemed to team us up with a girl twice our size when it was time to do rescue swimming. If you could pass these tests you were good.

July 19th was the feast of St. Vincent and we celebrated the entire day in the pool. Races in the pool in the morning were followed by a box lunch in the Grove. There were more races in the afternoon. The big show was in the evening. Everyone got to show off their swimming and diving talents. One year two girls dressed in a costume to look like a horse, then they went off the diving board, stripping off the costume as they dove in. There were always clowns that did a belly flop or a cannonball of the board, splashing the entire audience gathered around the pool. The Sisters' cornettes got wetter and more wilted looking as the show went on.

Although many of the girls could swim and dive like professionals, each year Irene Connery was the unchallenged aquatic star. She could swim faster and farther than anyone. She had power. She had style. Jackknives, one-and-a-halves, she dazzled us. Irene's swan dive was as graceful as the bird itself. Her back dive, skillfully executed on her tiptoes, backward on the edge of the diving board was as good as any professional diver or a diver in training for the Olympics.

Somehow Irene managed to get out of wearing her bathing cap. She had black curly hair. Her long slender legs further added to the impression that she was a graceful mermaid gliding through the crystal waters of an exotic tropical lagoon, rivaling Esther Williams in an MGM production. The only thing that ruined the vision of a graceful Esther Williams performance was Irene sticking out her tongue at her audience just before she executed a dive, or when she came up for air after plunging into the pool. She was such a clown.

The grand finale of the annual pool extravaganza was always a water ballet by the high school girls. This was timed to start when the sun went down which highlighted the special lighting and the candles balanced in their hands by the swimmers. It was a fitting celebration for the feast of St. Vincent.

We were on an outing, using a charter bus to take us to the sight, and this was our cheer for our hero when we arrived at our destination:

"Two. Four. Six. Eight. Who do we appreciate?
THE BUS DRIVER!
Stand him on his head, stand him on his feet.
The bus driver, bus driver, can't be beat!"

Somehow this cheer, which we shouted at the top of our lungs, just could not possibly redeem us from the hours and hours of horrific deafening abuse we bestowed upon the bus drivers who were unfortunate enough to have to drive us to and from our numerous outings.

The outings were usual in the summer and almost everyone came—all of the five groups of 20 girls each—but somehow we always managed to fit into just one chartered bus.

Before each take off, there was a prayer to St. Christopher for a safe journey and a few extra quick prayers to various other saints we would entrust our lives to that day. We ended with a prayer to St Vincent de Paul.

When the bus was down the road a piece and out of Sister's sight, the real fun began. The one-hour drive to Glen Echo Park, Maryland, probably felt like it took a lot longer for the poor driver after the first round of "A Hundred Bottles of Beer on the Wall" was sung.

A couple of the girls would walk up and down the aisles of the bus like barmaids, taking orders, passing imaginary beer around on imaginary trays. Meanwhile the rest of us drank the imaginary beer and acted drunk. When we got down to the last beer we were all drained but someone would start up another chant.

My favorite was one we sang especially while standing in traffic next to a group of teenage boys in a car or just before we arrived at our destination and wanted to announce who we were. To the tune of "Ta-rah-rah-boom de-ay" or "It's Howdy Doody Time," we sang this song:

"We are St. Vincent girls, we wear our hair in curls.
We wear our dungarees way up above our knees.
We wear our brothers' shirts, we wear our fathers' ties.
And when we go outside, we are surprised."

Almost always, one girl could not contain herself and would turn around, lift her dress and show off her panties after the line "we are surprised" and everyone, without skipping a beat, in perfect time to the music, would shout "woo woo" at the end of the song.

When we arrived at Glen Echo, we were turned over to one of the older girls, a girl in high school. It seemed unfair to drag her around to the kiddie rides but most girls did not complain too much since they could still pal around with their best friends and still watch their little charges. But they were completely unsupervised by an adult.

They were in charge and they let us know it.

One of the benefits to being with the older girls was food. Well, money bought the food and they always had lots of spending money. If we cooperated and acted at least half human, they would buy us one of Glen Echo's specialties—cotton candy, candy apples or the East Coast's freshest French fried potatoes. They would even splurge and treat you to a game of skee-ball when they were feeling generous.

We had precious little spending money from our "book," Sister's little wonder of accounting in the form of notebook pad. So I never wasted my cash on the games of throwing darts or pitching balls to win prizes, which never challenged me. I gravitated toward the "guess your age" booth where some articulate, obnoxious middle-aged con artist, speaking through a microphone, hurled insults and obscenities to the passing suckers who were sheepishly lured to his area. Now this was a show worth watching. And I never looked my age, always older, so I always walked away with a kewpie doll on a stick or some other tacky prize.

But I was really one of the younger girls, and if an older girl said so, then you did it—you had to ride the big roller coaster, front seats of course, whether you were afraid or not. There were lots of other rides—the big airplanes, bumper cars, and "the Whip." You had to ride the Round Up, one of the newest rides at Glen Echo, where you are standing, strapped in, but you are really held up by centrifecal force.

They reminded you to keep your mouth shut or it would stay open during the ride because of the speed of the ride. Lots of kids threw up on this ride. They just couldn't keep their mouths shut—and the vomit flew out of their mouths, but was kind of suspended in mid air, kind of like sparklers that just light up and then disappear into nothingness!

They reminded you to keep your mouth shut for other reasons, like when they wanted to smoke behind one of the buildings. Or when they just happened to run into one of their boyfriends.

Shutting up was the easy part. The older girls changed their attitudes when they were hooked up with boys and we got away with a lot more. Bribes with an older girl were so much fun—lots of blackmail going on. Everybody got to do exactly what they wanted and nobody got hurt.

Well, I do remember one girl being hurt. She had a terrible crush on one of the boys but the boy liked someone else. We tried to cheer her up by getting her to stand in front of the Glen Echo. Laughing Lady. Remarkable how much she sounded like Sister Alma. I guess we were just too young to know it would take more than the laughing lady to help her get over a broken heart.

Later on, we rode the Cuddle Up, one of the rides like the Tea Cups at Disney World. You could never verbalize your feelings but these were magic moments. Maybe it was the fact that the little girls were trying to connect with the big girls, and the big girls wanted to be looked up to, sort of like sisters. Or maybe it was just that we liked the name of the ride so much—the "Cuddle Up"—but those days made us feel very good, all warm and fuzzy, like a family being tossed around in a crazy, amusement park ride and cuddling up to each other.

For the cost of the regular fare, plus a surcharge to go into the State of Maryland, you could take the # 40—Cabin John streetcar to get to Glen Echo Park, something we did many times while home for a weekend. Riding the streetcar over the old, rickety trestles by Georgetown was as thrilling as riding the roller coaster inside the park. They had screechy brakes on the streetcars that we were told could stop-on-a-dime.

The streetcars stopped right in front of the amusement park. At night, the famous art deco lighting around the park was showcased, especially at the entrance way. It sort of matched the ambiance of the Spanish Ballroom inside the park. The entire park was like a huge town fiesta, with the huge letters at the entrance to the park that lighted the sign that could be seen even from a distance.

Glen Echo.

The highlight of the entire park was the Dentzel Carousel. It was graced with ornately handcarved and decorated graceful horses, lions, ostriches and tigers, and chariot-style seating. There was the magnificent pipe organ, maybe 12 feet tall, with its merry music that could be heard throughout the amusement park. They played familiar tunes but they sounded so majestic coming through the fabulous pipe organ and gave an air of elegance and majesty, as though you, on your chosen horse, were leading the parade of animals and performers of the Barnum and Bailey Circus.

The Crystal Pool was a relatively new addition to Glen Echo when we went in the late 1950s. Although we had a pool in the Grove at St. Vincent's, it was always a real treat to be able to swim there because Glen Echo's Pool was no ordinary pool. It was huge, at least four times the size of ours, with an island at one end that divided the 3 to 4 ft. area from a deeper end. There was a 20' high sliding board always piled with kids going up the ladder, some so scared they wet their pants, but who noticed. By the time you got to the top there was no turning back. Lots of kids chickened out but were pushed down the slide anyway. No one was going to lose his or her place in line and no one was going to budge to let you back down the ladder.

There was another pool just for diving with two diving boards, one a regulation size, the other a high dive. This is where a St. Vincent girl could really shine. We were better swimmers and divers than the average. MM and I felt an added bonus because everyone thought we were Hawaiians, something to be proud of in a swimming pool. We did not have to wear bathing caps and could let our long black tresses free in the water and we definitely did not have to put on suntan lotion. Our golden tans and pride carried us a long way at the Crystal Pool.

Every year we went to Marshall Hall, another huge amusement park. We would board a boat—the Wilson Line on Maine Street Southwest for the slow cruise which made a stop at Mount Vernon on the Virginia side and ended up at Marshall Hall in Maryland. The first building to the left when you got off the boat was a penny arcade game place that had slot machines. There must have been an age limit but no one ever checked. It did not matter much since we had very little cash. They gave us tickets to ride everything after enjoying a huge meal in the wooded picnic Gove to the rear of the park.

Another annual event was the picnic at Pierce Mill in Rock Creek Park. Children from all of the homes around the City were invited— St. Joseph's for Boys, Junior Village, Good Shepherd, German Orphan Home and more. There could have been two to three hundred children who attended. We always stuck close by the guys from our brother institution, St. Joseph's Home for Boys, and felt as though together we were by far the "coolest" kids, none of us orphans, all of us brilliant and coordinated, ready to dominate any physical or mental contest.

We participated in relay races according to age. When they provided the huge picnic lunch complete with hot dogs, baked beans, ice cream and candy, the *starving orphan* in us reared its head shamelessly, and we ate second and third helpings till we could eat no more.

On a stage in the center of the park there was entertainment like sing a longs or magic shows. One year Dick Mansfield from the D.C. Police Department did his safety demonstration using clever artwork on a flipchart. At the end of the performance, everyone sang with him.

"We're safety cavaliers, we use our eyes and ears. We look both ways, then cross the street, we're safety cavaliers."

Then everyone's name would be called and they would be given a gift like a Brownie Scout camera, an Erector set, a doll, a bingo game or a jump rope. It was like Santa giving us toys at Christmas time.

One year Judy Garland's daughter, Liza Minelli, appeared on stage. She did not perform, and we thought she was a little strange, so quietly staring off into space. Someone called her a sissy. We all affirmed she was a sissy, after she was seen carrying around a doll baby. Guess we found it peculiar that she was our age. Most likely, we just envied her—shiny ponytail and beautiful, frilly ruffled dress, and the fact that Judy Garland probably sang *Somewhere Over the Rainbow* to her every night. Maybe she was okay after all.

No one can drive in front of the White House anymore. It's blocked off to vehicle traffic. But one steamy summer morning during the "dog days of summer" in 1962, Mr. Sam, who drove the girls in an old panel truck for St. Vincent's, drove us down Rhode Island Avenue, zigzagged through 17th Street to avoid Lafayette Square, and dropped off 15 young ladies directly in front of the residence at 1600 Pennsylvania Avenue.

We were going to visit the home of the President, so we dressed in our best Sunday clothes, complete with pillbox hats, white gloves and, many of us in four-inch high heels. Most of the young women who walked in front of the White House in those days were "dressed to kill," donning their finest outfits on parade down Pennsylvania Avenue. Why not us? And why not complete the outfits with white gloves, *before* climbing down from the truck!

It was not an easy drop-off for Mr. Sam. He had to personally assist each "little lady," as he called us that day, over the three-foot railings of truck and down to the sidewalk. He was truly a gentleman and helped us unboard as modestly as possible under the compromising circumstances.

"You look like a million dollars," he said to each of us as he proudly held our hand and walked us from the truck to the curb. After our tour, Mr. Sam was waiting for us in front of the White House in the big green panel truck He had one side of the rails pulled out to make it easier to climb in the truck, then drove us back home in style.

On a beautiful but humid summer day, a fashion show was given at the Shriver family home in Rockville, Maryland. We were not in on the planning by Sargent and Eunice Shriver and other Kennedy family members, of course. The show was for the benefit of the girls of St. Vincent's Home and School, and we were treated like honored guests. Someone must have heard our prayers. It seemed someone was concerned about the pitiful clothing budget we had and decided to do something that would make a difference.

It was a wonderful occasion, with the fashion show and the lovely catered meal outdoors on the lawn. When the heat and humidity become unbearable, we went inside to wander around the house. Seated all alone near a window, engrossed in a book was an adorable, precocious little girl who invited us in to read books. I believe she said her name was *Maria*. We chatted with her and she seemed to like the idea that we were not little kids and not yet adults. We asked if she wanted us to read her a story.

"No. I'll read one to you," she said, picking out a picture book and, turning the pages slowly, she told us a story. We were not sure that she could actually read, but she was animated and we enjoyed the show. Afterward she curled up against the window quietly and went back to her own book. Apparently the fashion show and all of the day's activities tired her. We did not know the names of any of the other children that were running in an out of buildings. We figured she was one of the Kennedys.

We had heard that the Kennedys did a lot of charity work. This day showed us they had their own special flair. They didn't simply write out a check. They become involved first hand.

On another occasion, we were invited to go swimming at the Kennedy's home—Bobby and Ethel of Hickory Hills in McLean, Virginia. Of course we had our own pool, but this was a very special day for us. Mrs. Kennedy allowed us to be as disruptive as any children, running in and out of the house, throwing towels and people into the pool.

Jamie remembered seeing horses on the property and asked for permission to feed them. The staff was not around and she found Bobby Kennedy instead, who handed her some apples and gave her permission to feed the horses if she did it right. Inside the house was an entire wall of black-and-white photographs that formed a family gallery. In the garage, the snow skis were lined up according to height.

The Kennedys opened their pool, their home and their hearts to children from other organizations as well on Mondays and Tuesdays. Wednesdays was reserved for the girls of St. Vincent's and Thursdays, for the boys of St. Joseph's Home. Fridays, it was said, the Kennedys went to Hyannis Port.

As much as the Sisters loved the Kennedys, we were surprised they rarely went with us on many of these outings. So often they forfeited their own desires for our added entertainment.

The Generosity of Volunteers

"A Brother jumping rope" could be a title for a rap song in the new millenium. But at St. Vincent's in the 1950s, a Brother jumping rope had to be taken literally. A local order of Catholic Brothers came to St. Vincent's several times a week to help us with homework. We never realized exactly where they came from but looked forward to their help. They were especially good at arithmetic and could help you study the day before a test.

Afterward they always had time to play a game or two in the Grove. They played "kick the can" or they pushed us on the swings. They'd even play basketball, making a game out of the multiplication tables while they helped us dribble. A funny scenario was a Brother turning the rope for us when we played jumprope. Funnier still was a Brother trying to jump into a double-Dutch game, holding his brown wool frock high to avoid the rope. They'd have the time of their lives listening to our jumprope songs. Then we would create chaos; we'd get that look in our eyes, give each other the sign and yell, "SKIN!" The girls turning the ropes would go at double or triple speed. We always tangled them up in the ropes and had to stop the game because everyone was laughing so hard. They were good sports.

The Ladies Auxiliary of St. Vincent's was always planning events that would benefit the the social programs for the girls of St. Vincent's in very specific ways. The backbone of their grandest and most memorable event was their annual card party held at the Daughters of the American Revolution on Massachusetts Avenue. A special program was printed each year that thanked the business and personal sponsors of St. Vincent's and acknowledged the special help of the volunteers. The name that appeared on every single program was Rita McAuliff. But the kudos extended to Rita were shabby indeed for the amount of effort she put into these activities over the years.

Thanks to Rita McAuliff and many other volunteers who worked tirelessly throughout the year, another annual event took place. The famous "Spaghetti Dinner" became synonymous with St. Vincent's. The aroma of the spaghetti sauce, cooked days ahead of time, flooded the entire building. The Ladies Auxiliary and other volunteers cooked, the girls who lived at St. Vincent's served and the alumnae had an opportunity to get together to relive old times. The small fee charged for dinner probably added considerably to the coffers of the special funds for the residents of St. Vincent's.

For 12 little girls at St. Vincent's, the ABCs of dance were introduced to us in 1958 by Miss Anne Moorehouse from Georgetown, Washington, D.C. Anne came as volunteer, like so many other young women from Trinity College. Most of these student volunteers helped us with homework or played outdoor games and sports with us. But Anne Moorehouse, with her straight hair usually pinned in a neat bun, had her own niche and her own following—she taught us ballet. We called our group, the ABCs— "Anne's Ballet Club."

We were 11 and 12 years old and most of us thought that we would be dancing on *pointe,* in toe shoes, within a few weeks. MM and I had attended a class under the tutelage of Leon Fokine at the Fokine School of Ballet on Columbia Road. I loved every torturous moment of practice. MM hated it. We knew intimately that we were in for more sweat, pain and discipline than mere glamour and fame.

Anne had us practice the five positions with our feet, then adding cumbersome stretching exercises and graceful movements of our hands and arms. Months later we graduated to the *assemble, pirouette* and *echappe.*

She would give us a break every once in a while, and let us do some solo, free-form style dancing all around the floor. She would play records that ranged from traditional ballet musical like Swan Lake and Giselle to jazz and tap dance tunes. She realized that there were no Pavlovas in the group, and we needed some little stress-relieving activities to keep us motivated and to stay focused on ballet. So after a few precious minutes of down time, she returned us to our alternative "barre," the windowsills along the walls, and the folding chairs in the middle of the auditorium, back to the business of ballet dancing.

Anne decided she would show off her ballet students and created her own ballet. It was similar to *Coppelia,* the famous ballet about a doll that comes to life. With music mixed and snatched from the works of Debussy, Delibes and other, Ann called our ballet *The Magic Toyshop.* I was the star, the doll in the toyshop that came to life one evening after the old shopkeeper closed for the night.

We all had important characters in the ballet. There was a Calico Cat, played by best friend Mary Elisabeth Holmes, and a Gingham Dog, played by MM, a jack-in-the-box, a toy soldier and a whole assortment of board game characters.

There were several younger girls who were dressed in costumes that looked like stuffed animals or toys. One girl even wore a big black box that said MONOPOLY, while another girl with a sailor cap had a box hanging from her body that looked like a boat.

Anne narrated the story on stage, then excused herself every few minutes to either change the record player, brush someone's hair, pin a costume together, give cues, push a little ballerina on stage or demonstrate a dance step to a girl in a stupor.

Our 19-year-old ballet mentor had my total commitment. As a reward for being her second set of hands and feet, she put my name on the program followed by the magical word "choreography." We felt as though our career in the performing arts was launched. Sister even bought roses to give to Anne and we did several curtain calls that day. The show was a huge success.

The bigger, more elaborate show that followed *The Magic Toyshop* was a sad one. Anne Moorhouse married Fred Lekson at Holy Trinity Church in Georgetown. She quit college, which did not really faze us one way or the other. But she moved to Cleveland, which devastated us. Her parents invited us to their home for dinner before she departed for Ohio. It was a wonderful visit and her fiancé Fred was flattered when we sang him a popular song with the words that were meant just for him.

"We're havin' fun sittin' in the back seat, kissin' and a huggin' with Fred....Seven little girls sittin' in the back seat. All of them in love with Fred."

But the day at the Moorhouse home came to an end, and we began to feel the pain. Anne left town. Just like so many people had done to us before in our young lives, she was gone, too.

A classmate of Anne's from Trinity, Rosalie Manasseri, had been volunteering her time at St. Vincent's too. She paid special attention to those of us who had been taking ballet from Anne and she helped us to realize it was not the end of the world. There were still good things to look forward to.

Rosalie introduced us to something almost as wonderful and certainly more practical than ballet—PIZZA! Imagine not having your first slice of pizza until you are 11 or 12 years old. Pizza has to be an all-American food, and we had been deprived up to this point. We went to the Manaserri's home in Marlow Heights, Maryland. Mrs. Manaserri did everything from scratch and we spent hours helping her make the dough, watching it rise and making the sauce. It smelled authentically Italian. The end result was the tastiest food I had ever eaten. And we could have as much as we wanted—a rare treat for a girl from St. Vincent's.

Another traditional event at Thanksgiving time was the annual U.S. Marines' Toys for Tots Gala! We were invited guests, all 300 of us from various homes and agencies, at the Naval Gun Factory by the Navy Yard for a Thanksgiving dinner complete with all of the trimmings, from *young-roasted-Tom-turkey*, as it read on the elegantly printed menu given to each child, to mashed potatoes with gravy, cranberry sauce, buttered green peas, fresh-baked rolls with butter to freshly baked pumpkin pie.

After dinner, we were escorted by the Marines to a huge

auditorium where we saw a spectacular variety show with music from the Navy Band. When each child's name was called, we proceeded to the stage at the front of the auditorium to receive a Christmas present from Santa Claus.

As we boarded our buses to go back home we were presented with another gift—a goody-filled stocking, almost as tall as we were. We continued to sing the Christmas carols that lingered in our heads, feeling the excitement of the holiday season in the cold night air. For the little girls of St. Vincent's, this event was confirmation that there was a Santa Claus. It was a time to be grateful for the kindness of strangers during the holiday season and to enjoy an evening out, an opportunity to stare at handsome young soldiers in uniform. We could almost believe in elves too.

Several weeks before Christmas, we were given the opportunity to buy and give gifts for our families and friends through Station WTOP's "Dollars for Orphans" Program. Children from all of the area homes and orphanages were given $5.00 each to shop for their parents and siblings at G.C. Murphy's. One year it was held at Neisner's, a local five-and-dime, though it was not nearly as successful at this location. Murphy's had a huge luncheonette, which doubled as a stage for the Master of Ceremonies and the entertainment. The amount of money given to each child was increased over the years for inflation.

MM and I shopped together one year, supervised by a volunteer who monitored the shopping of about five other children.

"What do you want for Christmas, Nita?"
"A goldfish. But don't show me. I want it to be a surprise."

MM bought a pair of gloves for Dad for about $3.00, and a bunch of 25-cent items with the rest of her money. She told the volunteer that all of the stuff was for her sister, since she only had one sister, but she couldn't let me see it. The volunteer commented that her sister was lucky she would be getting so many presents. She had her packages wrapped and MM was done.

I never did get the goldfish. She told me it would have died on the bus. And I would have needed a bowl and fish food, which she didn't have money for. I never got any of the other junk she said was for me either. Guess she kept all of the good stuff.

But I was not surprised. It was her tradition to dupe me on gifts. On my birthday, which is also her birthday, I used to give her a decent gift, no matter what it cost me. I would always find something nice for her. She'd thank me, then wrap it up and give it back to me. Then she added, "if it's too small for you" or if "you really don't like it" it would be no problem to give it back to her! She always volunteered her thoughtfulness.

A False Fire, Then Home for Good

About six weeks after school started in the seventh grade, I created some new problems for me and MM. I do not know why what I believed to be a simple "event" became an enormous "incident." For some reason, it seemed we were always in trouble at that point. It must have been the age.

One weekend, MM and I and several other girls from St. Vincent's walked to the Edgewood Playground. Just down the hill and turn left, out Edgewood Street to Fourth.

This was one of those typical things we would do if we did not go home for the weekend with Dad. We looked forward to walking to the neighborhood playground for a few hours of skating or basketball, just like other children our age. Naturally, we wanted to be as "normal" as possible. Naively, we assumed that we would blend in with the neighborhood, sort of like "passing," so that no one would know we were from St. Vincent's, despite our dresses-only attire and "sturdy" Catholic school-girl shoes that fit snugly in our ballbearing skates.

Along the way to the playground, several blocks from home, there was a fire alarm box mounted on a five-foot high iron post in the sidewalk. Nothing out of the ordinary. Oddly, this day I was very curious. I do not know why I had to get special attention from the Fire Department of the District of Columbia. While waiting for the little girls from the younger group to catch up to me at a corner, something compelled me to pull down the handle on the box, so I did. I was disappointed that nothing happened. So I pulled the alarm again.

All of the sudden, from both sides of Fourth Street, fire engines, a total of four, and a few police cars, came rushing to the scene of an expected fire. Sirens blaring from both sides of the street, the piercing noise brought the full neighborhood out of their houses and onto the porches and sidewalk.

Panic gripped me and I knew I was in trouble. Everyone knew I had done it. Everyone else had been curious about the box too but I was the one—a 7th grader, who should be setting a good example for the little ones—I was the one who pulled it. A solemn-looking cop took down information that I nervously provided. He wanted to know my name. My cohorts were wonderful—they shouted out my name and even spelled my last name for them. Not surprisingly, he knew the address of St. Vincent's. He continued, exasperatingly, to question me about my motive for pulling the fire alarm. I had no answer for him about that. I just did it.

The girls of St. Vincent's, seeing my frustration, turned on the loyalty when we got back home. Girls tried to protect me from the policeman who was waiting for us when we arrived and from Sister Josephine, the Superior at that time. One younger girl even said she had pulled the fire alarm, hanging her head in shame. My sister and her pals started throwing rocks at the police car and were taken upstairs to their group on the second floor by another Sister whose expression merged the embarrassment and anger at the day's events.

It became a long evening. Upstairs in our dormitory I knew the girls in my group were admiring me for my "guts" in doing something so forbidden. My stomach was twisting in knots and my head ached with pain. I felt like I had literally LOST my guts! I barely breathed for hours, fearing the wrath of the Sisters, but mostly the wrath of my Dad, when they got around to calling him.

Bear the burden of your actions. This was one of the many self-improvement lessons we were accustomed to hearing. There were severe consequences being tallied up as a result of the incident of the fire alarm box and a few other minor transgressions involving MM. They just seemed to stack up against the two of us.

In the days that followed, Sister Josephine questioned the Sisters in charge of our respective groups about the reasons we were at St. Vincent's. We were not orphans. Dad did not want us to be adopted or placed in a foster home. Moreover, we had family. We were barely subsidized by Catholic Charities; Dad paid a very high percentage of the real cost of being placed at St. Vincent's. We had a stable, family-oriented place to go every weekend.

Regrettably, the push was on to have us leave St. Vincent's, and within weeks we were gone.

Part Two:
A Quick Escape

A Chaotic Interim

When we left St. Vincent's in the Fall of 1958, we went to live with Aunt Edna. MM adjusted well to living with Aunt Edna. She was happy to be reunited with the family. We had lived at St. Vincent's from June 1952 to October 1958. I had adjusted so remarkably to St. Vincent's and to our institutional life. So when we left St. Vincent's I was lost. I loved my family but St. Vincent's had been my home and I felt uprooted again.

The Rillon family lived in a duplex house in Oxon Run Hills, Maryland. Ralph who was born shortly after we first entered St. Vincent's, was now six years old and in the first grade at Green Valley Elementary School. Janice was a freshman at Suitland High School and Ray was a freshman at Montgomery College in Takoma Park. MM attended the sixth grade at Green Valley and I was a seventh grader at Benjamin Stoddard Junior High School in Marlow Heights. We also had another cousin living with us—Joseph Collins. His father, Aunt Edna's brother Olson, made good money at a brewery in Baltimore and sent Joe to Holy Family Catholic School. Joe hated going to a different school than his cousins. I envied him. Public school was a new and rather uncomfortable experience for me.

It was surely not the fact that I started my menstrual period at that time, for that was rather uneventful. We took showers every day after gym class and I would simply say "regular" and did not have to follow the line to the showers. My modesty got in the way. It was

147

about six weeks of claiming "regular" till I was found out and had to join in the undress-shower-get dressed party after gym. It was what everyone else had to do and it was what I reluctantly did as well.

Things were just not going well for me. It seemed at times that my poor vision was my primary problem. For several years in school I squinted to read the blackboard, avoiding the free government eye test they offered at school, knowing how badly I needed glasses. My vanity finally gave in to doing something about my severe myopia. Dad took me for an eye exam at Sammit Optical on F Street.

When I picked my glasses up and wore them for the first time, feeling as though I were wearing a magnifying glass that gave me "supersonic vision" like Superman, the glasses exaggerated the number of freckles on my face. Soon the real problems became clear. I noticed that downtown D.C. was dirty. Bums and drunks hung out on the street corners by Chinatown and all along F and G Streets. The stone and mortar on Old St. Mary's Church was a drab grey. The magnificent library at Ninth and New York was like a magnet that attracted a multitude of street derelicts and using the restroom under the building was like taking your life into your hands.

The glasses were powerful. Dad, who had been the most resourceful and accomplished human being to me, now gave the appearance of being just a "poor working stiff." Aunt Edna never lost the weight she gained from having my cousin Ralph. Still beautiful, still with gorgeous long blonde hair, she didn't quite resemble Marilyn Monroe the way I remembered her in my earlier childhood.

No one else in the house was a practicing Catholic except cousin Joe. If I wanted to go to Sunday Mass I had to make special arrangements to get there and to take the religion class, "CCD," short for Confraternity of Christian Doctrine, once a week. MM went to the Church of Christ with Aunt Edna and despite the nine people that lived in our house, I felt lonely and on my own when it came to a shared faith, something that was taken for granted at St. Vincent's. Aunt Edna kept encouraging me to join MM and my cousins at their church. She did not understand why anyone would wish to go to a Mass said in Latin when her church had lots of music and social events after the service to participate in. It would have been nice to combine the two church experiences—the social and the spiritual. She did not realize just how much it meant to me to be a part of the

Mass and to witness the most amazing miracle—the transformation of the bread and wine into the Body and Blood of Jesus Christ.

Aunt Edna reminded me that "Sister" was not looking over my shoulder and that religious practices should be done according to an individual's own conscience and own choices. She wanted the best for me and she could be so persuasive. So many Catholics were using those same words at the time and it seemed being a Catholic was a matter of choosing from a menu of beliefs and practices. Many things in the Church were changing—things like going to Mass on a Saturday evening instead of Sunday, not fasting before receiving Communion, not refraining from meat on Fridays. The Church was definitely changing and Catholics were making their own choices.

Somehow the conflicts at home got resolved rather amicably and I did make my own choices. I continued in the Faith.

We were experiencing the "real" world. MM and I had to go grocery shopping at the A&P or the Jumbo with Aunt Edna to buy food. No one brought it to our house in a big truck like they did at St. Vincent's. We learned to help with the cooking, cleaning even sewing and ironing. There was no Yale Laundry truck that would pick up our linens twice a week.

We had to make do with a pitiful "allowance" for our personal necessities. We rarely had candy money. We had to do babysitting or ironing to earn our spending money.

Everything was distorted and extremely up close. This was the real world. We had been living high on a hill, sheltered from every day life for six years.

For a brief phase we were reunited with Mom and stayed with her and her boyfriend, Pete Peralta. Pete owned a three-bedroom rancher in Seat Pleasant, Maryland. MM went to St. Margaret's School in Seat Pleasant with our cousins, the Dioso's. I attended St. Aloysius School in D.C. and had to walk about a mile from the house to the District Line to take the bus to school.

We had never known most of our family. Dad's family remained in the Philippines; we never met any of them. It was wonderful to find out we had a grandmother and she was still alive. Each week someone new would come to the house and claim to be a relative. It was about as hard to believe we had blonde girl cousins since we were dark skinned and dark haired from one aunt who lived up the street, and we saw on a daily basis, as it was to believe we had twin boy cousins from another aunt who lived miles away from Seat Pleasant that we had not yet met. We enjoyed the experience all the same, and hoped we would one day meet all of the relatives.

Our Grandmother Ila Mae, apparently suffering from dementia, also lived with us. Mom seemed to detest her own mother, perhaps because of her medical and psychological condition. Other family members told us Ila Mae had been educated in Cuba and, during pre-Castro days, had run an antique business, and traveled back and forth between the States and Cuba to purchase merchandise.

We could not understand the bad blood between our mother and grandmother. We adored our mother and considered ourselves fortunate to be reunited with her, despite her alcoholism and her ever-growing bad temper.

Mom was not much like a mother. She was referred to as the "gypsy" of the family by her brother and four sisters, who fed and cared for us when she would disappear for days at a time on a drinking binge with a new boyfriend. When she was feeling maternal, she would bring us along with her, like cherished jewels to show off to her drinking buddies at her favorite beer joints.

"These are my babies," she would tell everyone, as proud as punch to have us making the rounds with her.

We were in the back of her boyfriend Brooks' car, when Mom decided she would take over the steering wheel and pushed him out of the way to get in the right position to be able to use the pedals. The hours and hours of alcohol that saturated her system took over. She drove us from Corral Hills, Maryland to the Little Sisters of the Poor Chapel on H Street, normally a 15 to 20 minute drive, in about 10 minutes.

We froze to the back seat, afraid for our lives. She did not have a driver's license. We learned later that she had never driven a day in her life before this incident.

Deeply locked in our memories, the details still quite hazy, are the events of a particular evening in the bedroom of one of her boyfriends. MM and I awoke in the middle of the night and found three adults in the double bed with us. It was damp and clammy. Confused and groggy, crying like five-year-olds, we were told to go sleep on the couch because we had wet the bed and they were going to change the sheets.

Bar hopping around her favorite haunts in D.C., she did karaoke before karaoke existed, with the two of us as part of the audience. MM even got up on the stage to sing one night, after she was forced to guzzle a few drinks. My little sister paid the price the next day with the worse hangover an 11-year-old body could tolerate, and did not go to school.

After one of Mom's traumatic break-ups with a new boyfriend, her boyfriend came to St. Aloysius School and "attempted" to kidnap me from my eighth grade classroom. It could hardly be considered an actual kidnapping, because when he called Mom on a payphone for the "ransom"—to go back with him—she hurled the worst sailor language at him and hung up. He did not mistreat me. He just apologized to me for what had happened and took me home to Seat Pleasant.

MM and Mom were gone when I got home. Pete was also gone. Mom accused him once, when he claimed he was doing overtime, of sleeping at his job at the Navy Yard just to avoid her. The next day I learned to cook. They all returned in three days.

Things returned to normal, as normal as could be expected, under the chaotic conditions at home. Pete never raised his voice nor a hand to my mother. As a matter of fact, he was so happy she came back to him after her short escapade, he gave her a gift of a silky mink coat from Gartenhaus Furs. He also told her he would be happy to cook our dinner every night rather than have her worry about what to serve.

Our lives had a somewhat regular beat. Regardless of what occurred at home, MM and I always had to return to school.

Sister M. Bernard was "older than dirt" and very likely aged *several more years* in the *one* year she taught my class in the eighth grade. She was determined to have writers, mathematicians and scientists graduate from St. Al's eighth grade in the Spring of 1960. She primed us for the test we took to enter a Catholic high school. As far as I knew, everyone passed the test.

St. Aloysius School's enrollment was dwindling and our class was one of the last graduating eighth grade classes. Sister M. Bernard boasted that she had drilled Dave Garroway in English and helped him with well-constructed sentences and compositions, and that was why he was so successful in his career which took him to television as the host of the *Today Show*. We found it hard to believe. Dave Garroway was pretty old in our estimation. And we figured he did not go to St. Aloysius either. And we thought Sister was a little prone to exaggeration when she wanted to get her point across to us. But she said she "did it for Dave," and she was determined to do it for us too. "No extra charge—it's all covered in the price of your parents' tuition bill!"

One of my eighth grade classmates at St. Al's was Sharine Platon. Sharine lived at St. Vincent's and she kept me abreast of who had left and who had come to St. Vincent's, and what was going on there since I went home for good. During a school holiday, I went camping with Sharine and her family. I had never camped before. They picked me up at school and we enjoyed the one-hour trip to "the country."

The next day the family got up before the sun rose, packed the car and threw all of us kids in the back of the station wagon still in our pajamas. I was confused. It seems the Platon family lived in Gaithersburg, Maryland and we were on our way to Deer Park Lodge in Garrett County, Maryland, another two to three hour trip ahead. They got a good laugh out of that one. The whole vacation I proved how out of place I was in "the country." I was very iffy on the whole outdoor experience and was glad to get back to "the big city" in a few days.

One of the boys from school, James Shanahan, "Jimbo" to his close friends, said he had a sister a year yonger than us who lived at St. Vincent's. I didn't know her but I would ask him how his sister was and how things were at St. Vincent's. He was the best looking boy in our class and talking to him about St. Vincent's was a perfect pretext for just spending time with him

In the eighth grade, "slam" books were popular among the girls. Using a shorthand tablet with the spiral ring on the top, you numbered the first page from one to about 36. This was the page where any student who filled in your slam book picked a number and signed his or her name. The name of each kid in your class would go on the following pages, one name per page. The name was underlined. You would have the kids write a comment, good or bad, about each person, underline the remark, then place their number under it.

If you happened to have a crush on someone they would probably not write anything in your book that gave this away. But you could look in everyone else's slam book to find out who had written what about you. Not exactly a subtle way to figure out the latest puppy loves going on in the class. Usually a person would keep the same number for everyone's book. This made it easier to check out who liked you, who hated you and and the low down on just how your classmates really felt about you!

Jimbo and I were both so painfully shy our friendship never developed beyond the confines of the school yard. But I must admit I stared at our graduation photograph many many hours and was flattered to be positioned near him for the photograph shoot.

Dad's boss died and left him money in his will. Mom thought it was $30,000 and made plans for how it should be spent. Before we knew it they were talking about reuniting. We even started looking at houses in Hillcrest Heights. It was nice to see Dad so happy. We would walk around singing some of his favorite songs—especially songs by Hank Williams like "Hey, Good Lookin'"—and he would grab Mom to dance with her. Her favorite was "Jambalaya." For a brief period of time, Mom laid off the bottle and we got to see a more domestic side of her personality.

Dad was happy when he picked up his inheritance check. He planned to use half to pay off his taxicab and the other half for a down payment on a rancher. When Mom found out the check was only for $3,000, she told him to "stick it where the sun don't shine!" The rest became history.

Mom's alcoholic lifestyle proved too difficult for everyone so we moved with Dad to an apartment in Southeast D.C. This experience was like jumping from the frying pan into the fire. It proved very difficult for Dad to raise two growing teenagers by himself. Our expectations were not high. We had just come from one of the worst situations for young girls to go through.

We learned to sleep with our clothes on when we lived with Mom. Ever vigilant, we needed to be prepared for her impetuous actions, like getting up at midnight to go out to a bar. We continued this because we were never sure if she were coming back to get us, something she threatened Dad with all of the time.

In the summer of 1960, just before I entered high school, the Rillon family and the Mondoñedo family drove to Atlantic City, New Jersey for a short vacation. We stayed in a very inexpensive tourist house that allowed cooking. It was all so beautiful. We loved the boardwalk and the beach and went to the famous Steel Pier to see the diving horse. We thought we had died and gone to heaven; we didn't want our vacation to end. On the way back home we drove through Delaware to visit Janice who was married to Wayne Watson. Wayne was in the Air Force and was stationed at Dover Air Force Base. They were expecting a baby in a few months.

The Watsons were planning a visit home in a few weeks and Janice insisted that I stay with her as my eighth grade graduation present. I enjoyed helping her around the house and I went out on my first date with a buddy of Wayne's who lived on the base. They didn't think anything of the difference in our ages—the friend was at least 20 years old and it was a double-date with them. They kept telling me about Elvis Presley and his girlfriend Priscilla and the difference in their ages and comparing our situation to Elvis' affair with Priscilla. It didn't really matter. Dad would not approve but he would never know. We went to see the movie *Psycho.* I felt very grown up.

In September 1960 I started high school at St. Patrick's Academy. MM went to Kramer Junior High and started hanging out with a crowd from the Anacostia Southeast neighborhood. She and Dad butted heads constantly. He tried to control her activities. She was feeling rather free and independent and played hookey from school several times a week. She ran away several times. Her friends kept her supplied in hamburgers and french fries and found a warm space for her in the laundryroom of some old apartment buildings in the neighborhood. It got to be too much of a power struggle between Dad and MM. Dad started looking for alternative care for us. Catholic Charities began to put their feelers out for some suitable living arrangements for us.

Around this time Dad caught pneumonia and almost died. It took him several weeks until he could get out of bed, several months until he recuperated fully. Meanwhile, he could not drive his cab and there was no money coming in for the essentials like food and rent. We were used to taking care of ourselves. But we were far too young to hold down a job. And we had never thought of living on our own permanently.

Dad had no known living relatives in the United States and we dared not go back to Mom's or any of her sisters. We were really like orphans at this point and our prospects for being "one big happy family" were very slim.

Streets of D.C.

Joseph Alsop's house in Georgetown was "party central" in the 1960s. His guest lists included great throngs of people—celebrities, politicians, artists. They were the brightest, the smartest, the most creative and the hippest people in Washington, D.C.

MM and I were privileged to see the "behind the scenes" function of the Joseph Alsop household on Dumbarton Avenue. Mary and Joe Castillon, my godparents, stayed at the apartment Mr.Alsop had built for them in the basement of the home he designed himself. It was a beautiful stucco-cinder block house built in the 1940s. There was not another like it in all of Georgetown.—a simply constructed house, but as elegant inside as any of the neighboring dwellings. You couldn't miss it as you drove down Dumbarton, for it was painted bright yellow.

During our occasional overnight stays there in Georgetown, it was always a special treat to see the aviary room where Mary's parrot, Bill, lived when he was not at their apartment on 4th Street. Bill spoke a few isolated words in Tagalog and Spanish, but got hung up most of the time repeating simply "Hello!"

We were reminded not to touch the harp in the living room, but it was okay to look around and to go outside in the garden, a garden without grass. The garden was an area completely covered over in small pea gravel with lush plants and flowers along its borders. You could sit there and look up, but surrounded by masonry walls you could not see the fabulous stained glass windows of Epiphany Church next door. We went to Mass there several times and enjoyed the beauty from the early Sunday morning sunlight shining through the windows of this tiny sanctuary, a very sacred spot.

We loved to hear my godparents tell us stories of the Alsop brothers' travels to places around the globe. Joseph Alsop's brother Stewart and his family lived in Georgetown just down the street. Both brothers wrote for the *Saturday Evening Post*. Joe would rattle off names, corrected by Mary's cleaner pronunciation, of the stellar guests he served for dinner. Not being familiar with the names of Ambassadors and politicians, we were all the more impressed when they mentioned the Kennedys. Senator John Kennedy and his wife Jackie were frequent guests at the Alsop home.

We met Mr. Alsop on one occasion which was not a particularly positive time. He noticed that my godparents, *José* and *Maria*, as he called them, were upset with MM and me. They had taken us to the Barnum & Bailey Circus and we got lost on the circus grounds. Instead of waiting there for them, MM and I took the bus back to the Alsops' house. We spent half and hour walking through nearby "P Street Beach," a place without an ounce of sand but plenty of sun worshippers dressed in beach attire. Mr. Alsop evidently had a great deal of affection for my godparents. He reprimanded us for making them worry. He had a commanding presence. We stood and took our scolding remorsefully.

There was a lot less tension when Mr. Alsop was not at home. We would run through the house, jumping on sofas inside, and dodging hits from the pebbles in the garden we threw at one another outside. Running in and out of the house made the birds in the aviary go crazy and the squawking got deafening after a few minutes. There was always a ample supply of toiletries and ladies' makeup in the downstairs bathroom which was fun to experiment with. But we were always reminded of whose house it was, and we never got too far out of control!

Frankly, we were told that this was an important house, that many famous people had made big decisions over dinner parties in the very same rooms where we played. We were more impressed with the freedom we had to meander from room to room studying the treasured artifacts and personal effects of the famous Mr. Joseph Alsop.

We preferred the trips to Mary and Joe's apartment near Chinatown. I was the eldest of approximately 20 godchildren, and Mary told me often that I was her most special godchild. Perhaps she said that to us all.

We knew that Mr. Alsop and his dinner guests must have been very spoiled from the pampering my godparents gave them for they were wonderful cooks. They had an ancient kitchen with a gas stove, so old that it was probably advertised in the original Sears Roebuck catalog. They made the most wonderful steaks and fresh asparagus, everything smothered in butter. Dinner was always served on the finest china. For dessert there was always the creamiest ice cream served in small lotus bowls. Several hours later MM and I would be starving again and Mary would roast popcorn on the stove top in an old-fashioned popcorn roaster and of course she would drench it down with gobs of butter.

Mary went to Old St. Mary's in Chinatown to pray the rosary once a week. It was broadcast on the radio. St. Mary's is a beautiful old church. At one side of the altar is a huge medallion with the words inscribed, "O Mary conceived without sin. Pray for us who have recourse to thee." My godmother would get so angry with us and place a handful of coins in the box when we lit votive candles without paying for them.

I had special intentions in those days. MM ran away to get married with a guy from our Dixon Street neighborhood. I must have thought the candles and prayers would save her from a bad marriage. Everyone else who married at age 15 ended up with a bunch of snotty-nosed little kids and was eventually divorced. But whenever I visited my godmother and attended Mass or the rosary broadcast at St. Mary's, I lit a candle for my little sister's salvation. Of course I used my own style of credit. After all I was just in high school myself and didn't make any money. The candles were plentiful. Sister said many times, "the Lord helps those who help themselves."

Jesus Saves! I knew this. I knew it because Dad said it was so. And there was a neon sign at 5th and H Street that flashed this message to all who passed when the lights of the neighborhood went on in the evening. We saw the sign every time we went to dinner at Wing's or "the basement, " a simple walk-down restaurant in Chinatown.

What a naïve little girl I was. Originally, I thought the sign was there because the building was a bank and the flashing sign was just a reminder that since Jesus saves, you too could stash your money there for a rainy day. Dad told me it was a "rescue mission," a place where "street bums," homeless men and women, could listen to the word of God and get an evening meal. I didn't believe him for the longest time, because the building looked like a bank to me. There was always a long line of people waiting outside of its entrance whenever we passed the building.

Dad stopped at Chinatown one day as he was driving me home from school. He went into the lottery "office," as he called it, to place a few bets. He stayed longer than I expected and I got panicky when I remembered that we were going to have a science test the next day at school. I had forgotten my book and thought I could borrow the book from my friend Joan Landolt, who lived in Mt. Ranier. My plan was to just drive up to her house, get the book and be back in Chinatown before Dad even knew I had been gone.

Driving looked so simple, and Dad's Chevy was an automatic. So I got behind the steering wheel and started the car. I had never driven before. I did not have a driver's license and I had never had a driving lesson in my life. Amazingly, the car followed my commands and despite slamming on the brakes too suddenly a few times, I was on my way.

There were too many red lights but with just a few turns from H Street, I was on Rhode Island Avenue, heading northeast to Mt. Ranier. Several people waved at me but my hands were frozen to the wheel and I could not be friendly at this time. Then I realized they were not waving, but "hailing" me. I put the *Off Duty* sign in the window. Dad did this often and it protected Bell Cab #147 from getting any tickets from the police. I crossed the District line and finally arrived at Joan's house. Joan was stunned but she loaned me her book.

"Are you sure you don't want me to go with you to take the driver's test sometime? You know you really shouldn't drive without a license."

"No. I don't need a license. My Dad takes me wherever I need to go," I told Joan, as I grabbed her book and got back in the car. Joan's father was a cab driver too.

The ride back through D.C. was smoother. I thought I was getting the hang of it. When I got back to Chinatown, Dad was standing at the corner of 7th and H talking with a policeman. Dad seemed relieved to see me. Nothing was said to me. Dad just told the policeman that I was his daughter and everything was okay. Dad must have been in shock. He didn't speak a word all the way home.

Native Washingtonians avoided downtown and the area around the national memorials and the "SW Mall" for fear of being mauled by an out-of-towner. Tourists took over the city from April through October. The "pilgrimage" began from the time the Cherry Blossom trees at the Tidal Basin gave signs of budding life, until the enormous trees along Rock Creek Parkway gave their annual slide show of brilliant color in the Fall.

Dad and the other "hackers" or "nickel snatchers" hated the tourists that came in April. They were the cheap ones. They were the ones with lots of children and very little money for a well-spent vacation. They were the ones who never tipped. And most of them drove to D.C. from some other place in the continental U.S. of A, so they didn't even use taxicabs.

People from New York City and cities larger than D.C. always complained that D.C.'s downtown was like a village center and there were not a lot of shops to choose from. I remember three distinct "downtowns."

The first was the Chinatown shopping area at 7th Street and H. There were many little furniture stores, whose window ads claimed to save you money, but in reality they charged you "an arm and a leg" because they extended you credit. They lured you into their store with any kind of a gimmick. They might have just marked down a beautiful lamp or picture that would look perfect in your home. It was affordable so you went in to investigate. Then they got serious and trapped you with an entire household of furniture that could be yours for just a few dollars a week. They never did the math for you that would have revealed the true payment per month or the grand total after a couple of years. Mom got caught in these consumer traps too often. At 7th and F, there was a woman who hung around just outside of Hecht's, playing guitar and collecting money in a little tin cup. She gave the appearance of being blind and took in lots of money from the throngs of shoppers going in and out of the revolving doors at the Hecht Company. But when she got a cupful of change or a few greenbacks she packed her guitar and bags and walked down the street to Central Liquors, without assistance and with no *visible* problem.

A second "downtown" was the "authentic" downtown on F and G Streets, from 7th Street through 15th Street. At 10th and F, Woodward & Lothrop reigned king of the department stores with its "Main" and "North" buildings that had everything from furniture, to clothing, a bakery, a restaurant and even fresh Velati's caramels in the candy department. On the first floor was a bonified travel agency — *Ask Mr. Foster.* There was a Mr. Peanut Shoppe across the street from Woodie's that was a landmark because of its steamed-up windows. You just followed your nose to find the shoppe.

At the corner of 14th and G, in front of Garfinkel's was the most amazing display of exaggerated body movement. A D.C. policeman directed traffic during the evening rush hour in this spot. He was at least six lanky feet tall. Hands, arms, and legs in the air and everywhere. Bowing with deep dramatic gestures in thanks for the cars that stopped to let his mesmorized pedestrians cross diagonally across the intersection. It was as well choreographed as a ballet. The whistle he held tight in his mouth reverberating his wordless commands relentlessly. Tourists would stand and watch him direct the cars and pedestrians like a director with a baton, controlling every movement in his orchestra.

The third "downtown" area was actually the start of "uptown" at Connecticut and K, the "Bohemian" sector of D.C. It was totally infested with the artsy folks referred to as the "Beatniks" in the 1950s and the "hippies" in the 1960s. This area extended all the way past Dupont Circle to the area where Connecticut Avenue splits into a "Y." Many a hippie wedding took place at the sight of the fountain in Dupont Circle. Pre-ceremony, the happy bride and groom would come up from the underground area where the streetcars used to pass, now the right-of-way for the Metro subway system. The right lanes traveling north on Connecticut Avenue become Columbia Road and lead to the Adams Morgan area.

The tourists that complained about the lack of good food surely overlooked the *Blue Mirror*, the wonderful diner on F Street with blue-mirrored tile on its façade. They exhibited some of the most luscious-looking strawberry shortcake, salads, and other food in the huge glass display cases that faced the street and flanked the famous front doors. The meals there stood up to the anticipation created by the displays in the windows and the prices were not bad either.

Downtown also continued the tradition of a five-cent cup of coffee at Sholl's Cafeteria on K Street and the Hotel Harrington at E Street. If you wanted a real Western-style "cowboy" breakfast, complete with ham, eggs and griddle cakes or silver-dollar size pancakes, there was the Copper Kettle on K Street.

Gallery's was just around the corner from St. Patrick's Academy. They carried a very comprehensive line of religious goods and books. We searched there often for small gifts we might give to Father Adler but never found anything appropriate in our price range. Each of the three downtowns had hundreds of chain and specialty shops, a multitude of ethnic restaurants and real drugstores—Schwartz on Connecticut Avenue and People's Drug Store at 10th and F. Anything you had money for could be bought within this two-mile strip of Washington.

One of the Filipino associations sponsored a beauty contest one year during the summer that I lived at the Hill's Maryland foster home. Dad entered me into the contest and picked me up for the dance. I had been doing a lot of swimming and had a huge "X" on my back formed by the bathing suit straps covering me from the sun. Dad did not tell me that the contest winners were chosen ahead of time before the pageant. I became known as "Miss X," a runner up to the Queen.

When I walked the runway in my lavender gown, the announcer said, "Miss 'X' is a mestiza (Filipino-Caucasian, not Spanish-Indian), who lives in District Heights, Merry Land. She is unable to get a suntan on her back." This got a lot of laughs but I didn't mind the fun poked at me. After all, I had gotten a new dress for the occasion. And I got to keep the tiara as a souvenir of the event for all my trouble.

Around the corner from the Greyhound station at New York Avenue was a little shop that sold wigs. Every length. Every color. Every style. Looking for some extra cash to cover my book bill at St.

Patrick's and other incidentals, I answered their ad in the window one day. They said they would pay "top dollar' for human hair. They examined my hair. It was jet black and poker straight. They said it could be dyed any color and curled to suit any style. They insisted it was Korean, the best type. How right Dad was when he told me to use olive oil on my hair after I shampooed. I did not argue, just cried a little after they braided it and chopped off my 20-inch mane pride and joy. I felt scalped and naked but I took my $100.

The crazies were on every street. It was good to go home.

Part Three:
Going Back Home

The Times They Are a Changing

Just like the lyrics to the Bob Dylan song asserted, "The times they are a-changin…" things were changing in the outside world. But we were somewhat sheltered from the black vs. white bickering that was escalating in the 1950s. When the 1960s rolled around it was no longer fashionable to expose your bigotry overtly. And people in D.C. were skilled at disguising their distaste for one's ethnicity, masking their bigotry with justifications like "That's what we called them at home but we don't really mean any harm by these words," or "Well, that's just the way I was taught."

The worst racial bias we experienced at home at St. Vincent's, actually only minor "slurs" to the extra sensitive girl, could not even compare to the hateful anger and vile language that was being hurled at minority groups in the outside world. Yet there were subtle hints of bigotry, or more appropriately phrased "discomfort" about the different nationalities at St. Vincent's. It seemed as though St. Vincent's had been "lily-white" for a long time and suddenly "those people" were being placed there. The digs were subtle, but they still cut like a knife when you weren't prepared for them.

Lovingly, with no real malice, African Americans were "colored,"and later became "Negroes." Native Americans were "savages" or just plain "wild Indians." Filipinos were "island people" and Italians and other Europeans, but not Irish, were just plain "immigrants." It was especially "cool" in high school to be Italian or to associate with Italians. We never knew much about Jewish people but always felt we would have been God's "chosen people" had we been born Irish—at least in the popular pro-Irish culture of St. Vincent's.

Perhaps it was more a sign of the times than actual bigotry. We actually all got along at St. Vincent's and out in our schools. Who knows. Perhaps it was because almost everyone was from some minority group. It was more of an asset to be aware of other cultures and customs. The perception was that making fun of other cultures merely meant that you understood that culture and it was flattering to that particular ethnic group to pick on them.

MM and I were a contradiction in ethnic pride. One day we would smear lemons on our skin to get rid of the freckles, for beauty and for ethnic authenticity. No respectable "half Oriental" had freckles. I rubbed my skin more vigorously to compensate for having at least 100 more freckles on my face arms and back than MM. The next day we could be found stealing Sister Alma's clothespins and putting them on our noses to force our noses to grow in a more flattering, thinner, definitively-Caucasian structure. Nothing worked.

It was impossible to stay out of the sun at St. Vincent's in the summertime. So we tanned beyond the hues of the other girls. We endured our freckled faces, flat noses, tanned skin and all of the perceived defects that came with such traits.

On the social side of the coin, it was gratifying that the other girls might identify you as a "go-between" or a "peacemaker" or someone who was "fair," because you were neither black nor white. Being fair was crucial in institutional living.

We always thought that Annette Funicello was the epitome of success for a descendent of immigrants. Her parents, of Italian heritage, were hard-working people who likely never expected the phenomenal level of fame and fortune Annette achieved. She was beautiful. She was talented. She was wholesome. She was even Catholic! We saw this and felt there was hope for girls of other nationalities. She was our idol and role model.

Miss Nora, as kind and as fair as she was to all of the girls, would not take care of the colored girls' hair. There were some volunteers who would periodically take the sisters to a salon to have their hair washed and "pressed." In between times she insisted that MM and I care for the four sisters' hair. We asked ourselves why. Because we were darker-skinned than the other girls? Did we have some special skill with hair? Were our little fingers more coordinated and nimble because of our race? Who knows?

We never really questioned it out loud. But really—what did we know about cornrows? Who would teach us how to use what looked like torture devices to make their hair smoother? Why didn't they have to suffer like we did, sleeping in the metal curlers every night, then sitting patiently the next morning while Miss Nora made our finger curls.

We didn't care. Doing their hair was just an extension of "our duty" and we usually did what we were told. When we developed a little more of our own hand-eye coordination, we learned to press hair, smoothing it with an electric comb that worked like an iron. We used the Vaseline and barrettes and ribbons and we gave Iggy, Mousey, Dortney and Bootsie, the "nappy heads," as they called themselves, the prettiest hairdos in all of Group One!

In the late 1950s there were eight Filipinas living at St. Vincent's. There were the Mondoñedo sisters, the Panganiban sisters who were in the high school group, and Gigi "Dena" Belisario and Amelia Peña, who were our age. Later two more sisters came to St. Vincent's. They were in a group for younger girls. None of us spoke Tagalog or any other dialect but MM and I were probably exposed to the language and culture most. Each 4th of July all of the Filipinos were invited to a special Mass said at St. Aloysius Church. This was followed by the Independence Day celebration and reception at the Philippine Embassy where we met the current reigning Ambassador. As the girls matured and entered high school, they tried to downplay their individual racial backgrounds. MM and I would stare and listen to Dad in amazement, always wondering why his accent, so thick, never smoothed out to sound more "American." We were embarrassed many times when shopkeepers could not understand him and would look to us for a translation of what he had just said to them in English.

Dad was an extremely humble and unassuming man and would

perceive other people's bad manners as them just being grouchy, or "getting up on the left side" (he meant the "wrong side") of the bed.

Sometimes some of of Dad's language struck us as funny, sounding very much like a "country bumpkin" would speak. They were cute and didn't bother us too much. "Take out the light," for "turn off the light." Or "take off your head" for "move your head." Unfortunately, most of the idiocyncricies of his speech made us thoroughly embarrassed. It drew more attention to us than we wanted.

I shared this with Sister at school one time and she reminded me that Christ went through similar circumstances. She said it was wise to "turn the other cheek" to those who did him harm. But "cheeky" behavior, downright hateful behavior, was how I perceived it. Worst of all, when someone responded to Dad with one of those cutting remarks and I was expected to just "take it," it made me feel as though they would think of me as being not-too-bright, that I too didn't get it and being "foreign" was the same as being unintelligent.

Those of us who had one or both parents from the Philippines, Iran or some foreign lands commiserated over our embarrassment at our parents' lack of social acceptability. There were times when we felt cursed, dealt a double whammy. Not only were we away from our families and living in an institution but we also felt we had "foreign, non-American" parents. Perceiving our father to be "non-American" was rather ironic when we remembered the years of military service he gave to the United States, years when they defended Americans from the harm of foreigners!

Martin Luther King Jr.'s "March on Washington" made a huge impression on me. Like most Washingtonians I stayed away from downtown when there was a rally or some political activity going on. That astonishing day in 1963 I watched the proceedings from the safe distance of the television set. But Dr. King's message was ingrained in my soul. Here was another "prince of peace" who had the courage to try to make racial changes non-violently. After this march I believed that race relations would soon improve.

One summer Dad received a letter from a young relative. We went to Georgetown University to meet him. He was Father Mondoñedo, a strikingly handsome visiting Jesuit priest from the Philippines. He took us on a tour and played up the fact that we were relatives when he introduced us around to people at the University. We hardly noticed Dad's accent that day. We were proud to be Mondoñedos and we were proud of Dad.

We've Got That SPA Enthusiasm

In my first year of high school MM and I moved in with the Hale family in District Heights—Dean and Myra Sue. They insisted that MM attend Catholic school with their children. They had four children and another on the way. We became built-in babysitters but we could not complain. We had a private bedroom which we shared and a very stable environment. But there were rules that had to be followed.

Finding it too restrictive, and too far away from her friends, MM ran away after a few months and looked for sanctuary in the old neighborhood. She was found living in a basement laundry room, eating whatever food her friends could scavenge together for her. Unaccustomed to the freedoms and liberties of a normal American teenage upbringing, I found it too loosely structured. Living in the suburbs was a huge adjustment for me too. Suffice to say, there were too many "cultural" differences. We will leave it at that.

Aunt Edna offered to take MM back to live with her. It was there at Oxon Run Hills that MM met and married a neighbor from across the street. He was six years older but it seems no one in our family has ever cared about such trivial matters. He had a job. She continued on in high school until she had her first baby.

After two complicated years of living in two different homes and another year in the Hale's foster home, I returned to St. Vincent's. I had missed the Sisters and the girls. I was happy to be back home!

Going to St. Patrick's Academy at 10th and G was a decision I made quite easily when I was in the eighth grade at St. Aloysius. We took an all-day exam to qualify for entrance into one of the many Catholic high schools in the District of Columbia.

My choices were three: Holy Trinity in Georgetown, because this was where my ballet teacher was married. It was also near my godmother's place of work, also where she resided, and she had asked for my help after my godfather died. Notre Dame, because this was the obvious choice. St. Aloysius School had the same order of nuns and was located in the same school complex on North Capitol Street. St. Patrick's, because Dad had always told me he could not send me to college. St. Patrick's had an excellent business curriculum and he hoped and prayed I would take the Civil Service exam and become a secretary in one of the many federal agencies right in D.C.

Dad's attorney and friend, Cornelio Lopez, also recommended I go to St. Patrick's. His secretary was a graduate of St. Patrick's and he was pleased with her work. I got into all three high schools, and was happy to choose St. Patrick's.

St. Patrick's Academy, a huge old Gothic building and complex, was in the heart of the City. Directly next door to our school was I.B.M.; our typing class windows, about an alley's length of six feet from our building, separated us.

None of us knew that just a few years after our graduation our school would close. Our beloved auditorium that served multi-purposes—basketball court, after-lunch "lounge," assembly hall, dances and proms—would be used as the site for public Shakespeare and other dramatic presentations.

Our "sister schools," were St. Mary's in Chinatown, and St. Cecilia's. Other all-girl schools were Immaculata, Immaculate Conception, Sacred Heart Academy, Trinity, Notre Dame and Elizabeth Seton. The boys' schools were Mackin, DeMatha, St. John's Military Academy, and Carroll High. St. Anthony's in Brookland was co-ed.

St. Pat's was run by the Holy Cross order. We had nuns for each class with the exception of one lay teacher, Ms. Heath, who taught History and Science. In senior year we had a part-time lay teacher who taught Art Appreciation.

We wore green wool blazers with crisp white piping along the lapel, and green wool skirts. A pair of white bobby sox and saddle oxfords completed our school uniform. In the warm months we wore mint green "shirt-waist" dresses.

"We are the Colleens, mighty, mighty Colleens.
Everywhere we go people wanna know
Who we are, so we tell them
We are the Colleens....."

St. Pat's had a basketball team that played the D.C. Catholic high schools, like St. Cecilia's, Notre Dame and Immaculate Conception. Other than the few games I watched at Georgetown University, basketball never really interested me much. It didn't quite have the appeal for me as cheering on the players to victory. So I tried out for cheerleading and got on the squad in freshman year. Joanne Giannini's mother made our cheerleading uniforms from a heavy wool fabric that pleated well. Our uniforms looked sharp—kelly green skirts and vests, long-sleeve white button-down blouses and black and white saddle oxford shoes. The first day of practice we made our own pom-poms out of a pack of green and a pack of white tissue paper and a little string.

"Dad, I made the team." I was so proud to tell him. "Look, we made our pom-poms today," I said, showing him my tissue-paper handcrafted masterpieces, one pom-pom wrapped in string on each hand.

"POM-POMS? Why? That is illegal! What kind of school is that? Is it not a Catholic (he pronounced it—Cat toll lick school—accent on TOLL)? What are they teaching you girls?"

It seems a *pam pam girl* means a hooker in Tagalog, Dad's mother tongue. How could I have known that. I had to do a lot of explaining until we finally arrived at the same understanding of the situation.

"That's great. I will try to come to your games to watch your team play basketball."

As fate would have it, in the four years I cheered, he never came to a game. I was more relieved than disappointed. I would have been mortified to have my father come to a game. No one's parents ever did this. Furthermore, he had a very legitimate reason not to show up for a game. It seems the traffic and the parking situation near my school at 9th and G Streets were a nightmare even back then. Being next to Woodward & Lothrop's, it was one of the busiest corners in the city.

Despite how much the basketball team practiced, and how hard we cheered them on, we *never* won a game. Not a single game! Not in all four years! We broke all of the records for losing games on our league, probably in all of D.C.

We did win one practice game with a high school that was outside our league and got a quick, unfamiliar taste of victory. But we were there to have fun and that's exactly what we did.

I did not have a patent on the name *Juanita*. There was another girl with the same name—Juanita Ricchuiti, who had a sister named Theresa DeVore. There was also another *half and half* (half Filipino/half American) in my homeroom—Cristita Purcarey. These three were by far the prettiest girls in our grade.

As a freshman at St. Pat's you were assigned to a "senior sister," a soon-to-be-graduated senior who "initiated" you into SPA with a month-long series of initiations such as making your senior sister a lollipop corsage that she could wear and eat all day or saying the "freshman pledge." The freshman pledge, a few paragraphs of prose that paid "homage" to your stellar senior sister, was meant to humiliate you in the worst way and was said on your knees.

Turnabout is fair play. We had had four years to get creative and when we became seniors we had our day in the sun. I was proud of myself for coming up with a unique idea. I commanded my freshman sister to go to the travel agency at Woodies across the street. The agency was called *Ask Mr. Foster*. She was supposed to very professionally and politely ask the agent some embarrassing personal question, totally unrelated to taking a trip. My freshman sister was from Spain. We had a slight problem communicating so I wrote it all down for her. She innocently went to her homeroom teacher to get help. The plan backfired on me. I was reprimanded for going against the initiation rule of restricting the activities to the confines of school.

Margaret Oliver loved Senator John Kennedy and we could not understand why she openly toted a Nixon sticker on her notebook. It was a bold thing to do in a Catholic school. Most of us at St. Patrick's were Democrats in spirit even if we could not yet vote. Understandably, we labeled Margaret a traitor. She explained to us the sign read NIX ON NIXON! You just had to read it correctly. We believed and envied her when she got a volunteer job downtown at Kennedy's Campaign Office.

"Hi, everybody, welcome to the *Milt Grant Show*! Today's special guest is none other than the beautiful and talented ANNETTE FUNICELLO. She'll be performing her new song this afternoon— 'Pineapple Princess.' But first, a word from our sponsor, Briggs Hot Dogs."

It was exciting being a "regular" on the *Milt Grant Show*. This was a one-hour dance program much like Philadelphia's popular show *American Bandstand*. Joanne Giannini, who was also a freshman at St. Patrick's and lived very close to me near East Capitol Street, told me they were looking for regulars for the show. Since *The Show* started early in the afternoon, students from the downtown high schools were especially recruited. We could always be there on time. The WTTG, Channel 5 studio was in the Hotel Harrington, next door to the Queen Bee Restaurant. We used to "hang out" at the Queen Bee until the show began.

We rated the new record releases, had guest celebrities, had dance contests and even broadcast the show from various locations around D.C., such as the ice skating rink in Virginia. We always got Briggs hot dogs to snack on since they were the main sponsors and of course we were given free Pepsis to wash the hot dogs down. "Uncle Milty," an enterprising man of about 35 to 40 years old, did the Briggs commercials himself.

About one day a week, "Negro" students from the area, a different high school each week, were invited on the show. I showed up with a couple of the other regulars on their day. The reverse happened one day on the "whites" day. Unfortunately, a big confrontation for an innocent little misunderstanding occurred.

The day we showed up on their show was handled at lot more smoothly. One couple from Roosevelt High School invited us to stay for the entire show. They told everyone "It's not a problem — they're okay, they're light skinned coloreds!" We did stay for part of the show. And we saw some dance moves that would have put the best white dancers, the regulars who thought they knew all the dance moves, to shame.

Being regulars on the show, we got to meet lots of popular singers — Annette, Fabian, Bobby Rydell, Bobby Darin and Paul Anka. I even became the President of the Melodaire's fan club, and tried to get other star-struck teenage girls interested in spreading the word about the group's music.

Annette had always been our very favorite singer. We followed her career from the Mickey Mouse Club to her popular "beach blanket" movies. MM and I read every teen and movie star magazine we could find that carried articles of photographs of Annette. It was such a privilege to finally see her in person.

But my most memorable "celebrity" encounter was when I met Johnnie Marino, a sophomore from Mackin High School. His cousin, Mary Lou, was in my class. Johnnie and his cousin Frank ran away from home one day. They ended up somewhere in the state of Florida. When they returned, severely punished but wiser for their experience, they were the most popular guys around the Queen Bee. I loved Italians from that day forward. Shelley Fabares song which was very popular at that time, *Johnny Angel*, had special meaning for me too, till finally Johnnie asked me out.

Dating was a new experience for me. And going steady with Johnnie, not something that pleased Dad, was exciting. He invited me to his prom at Mackin and after shopping for days for a prom dress, I was ready and looked forward to the big date. But almost as quickly as we had met, another girl came into the picture, and before long, she took my Johnnie away from me.

It was not long after they started dating that they also broke up. The girl and I became very good friends throughout high school.

When I returned to St. Vincent's in 1961 after having been gone almost three years, it felt like a real homecoming, although many of the girls I had known before had gone home for good.

In the few years since I had left, I had had my first boyfriend, first date, first kiss.

177

I remember being very popular for about a month. Everyone was fascinated with my diary, which Sister found going through my dresser one day. I never really knew if she actually read the diary. I used to share passages from the diary. The girls listened to every detail about my dates with Johnnie Marino, "makin' out" while slow dancing at the Saturday night dances at the Buckley Club at St. Francis Xavier School, cruisin' in borrowed cars up the "Avenue" to the Mighty Moe which was the name of the local Hot Shoppes Restaurant on Pennsylvania Avenue after the dance, feeding our faces on thick juicy Mighty Moes, onion rings and Orange Freezes. Then we would linger some more at the door of my apartment when Johnnie dropped me off. I detected a higher level of respect among my peers.

Everyone at St. Vincent's took the usual college-preparatory classes for a Catholic High School. This included, for most of us, at least two years of a foreign language, usually Latin, maybe another two years of French, and the usual English/Science/Mathematics/History core classes. For those of us from St. Patrick's, there were fewer of these standard classes and more business classes. The curriculum was very rigid; we could not choose what classes we could take, they were fixed and mandatory.

Another oddity at St. Patrick's was that we did not change classes. Each section stayed in their homeroom and with the exception of Sister Clarence Marie, who went to the typing room, the teachers moved around the school.

I loved Shorthand and Typing classes. We used Underwood manual typewriters. We had access to a few Royal and IBM electric typewriters in our senior year. Learning Gregg Shorthand was like learning a new language. As Sister Clarence Marie told us in our introductory classes in junior year, "It will come in handy one day."

Serving as coach of our school's basketball team, Sister Clarence Marie tried her best to lead us on to victory. While we never won a basketball game in my four years at St. Patrick's, Sister was extremely successful in coaching us in shorthand and typing classes. She pushed us to go beyond the required 45 words a minute in typing and 80 words per minute in shorthand to pass the Civil Service Examination for federal jobs. We were even able to take the Civil

Service Exam at school and receive the results directly from the Civil Service Commission on E Street.

Despite our somewhat less academic requirements at St. Patrick's, we were still required to go through the usual core classes of any high school, and we were bogged down with tons of homework in every class just like everyone else.

At home at St. Vincent's, Sister Bernard used to turned the lights out early every night. Jamie would often sit up under her blankets to study with a flashlight. This seemed too risky to me. Sister could walk into the dormitory with the slightest sound or see the light moving along the pages of your book and you'd be caught.

One evening Jamie and I talked about having to study for several exams. It was exam week at school and we wanted to do well. We knew we would have to stay up to study long beyond our curfew that night, burning the midnight oil. Many of the girls would stuff some clothing under the blankets of the bed to make it appear there was someone in the bed. Then they would tiptoe down the hallway and go into another room to study.

That night after Sister turned the lights out in each of the dormitories, Jamie and I got down on the floor on our bellies and scooted ourselves out of the dormitory area into the "study room," a room with individual desks for each girl located just beyond the living room. Sister could have caught us at any time in the study room and we would simply explain how much homework we had. Since we had pulled this stunt many times and never got caught before, we did not expect to be discovered this time. But we especially did not think Sister would find us still down on the floor crawling toward the study room.

"What are you girls doing?" Sister asked us. Busted! In all honesty, she must have had absolutely no clue as to why we were "crawling" along the hallway floor. After all, she had never found us in the study room.

"We're studying for exams, Sister." We were in big trouble, we knew, but looking up at Sister, the shock from the scene was too much for our eyes. We observed that Sister did not have time to put her cornette back on.

"It certainly does not look like you are studying. It would

behoooove you two to get back in your beds immediately!"

No one giggled the way the girls usually giggled when someone got caught by Sister. No. This time, everyone howled and laughed out loud.

I was in high school when MM gave birth to my precious little nephew at the "new" Providence Hospital which was in Northeast, very close to St. Vincent's. I took the bus to the hospital to visit MM. Her husband gave me a ride back to St. Vincent's, but waited for me while I made a quick purchase at People's Drug Store in Brookland. I bought a small box of cigars in honor of my nephew's birth, and smuggled them back to St. Vincent's in my oversized purse.

It was a few days before I could pass the cigars around to the girls in my group. I definitely had to do this "on the sly." Smoking cigarettes was not allowed of course. Smoking cigars might have gotten us in much deeper *kimchi*. The cigars lit up a lot easier than the quasi cigars we used to try smoking that we picked from the bean tree in the Grove. The cigars were gross but we were excited to welcome our baby boy into the family and into the world!

Wheels, Wings and Water

"Nita, the pot is ready. Get me the vinegar."

"Dad, I hate vinegar! Don't put that stuff on them."

"You have to put vinegar in the crabs to es-steam them. Hurry up, they're going to get out from the pot."

August was the best month for hard-shelled crabs from the Wharf on Maine Avenue. The vendors promised they were from the Carolinas. Dad liked it because there were plenty of female crabs with lots of eggs and they didn't charge more for them. We always got to the Wharf early to be sure we could buy the female crabs.

"Filipinos are cheap," Dad always complained. "They won't buy a whole bushel at a time; just a few dozen. But those 'foreign people' will es-snatch them up quick!" According to Dad, Asians, Africans and Latins were foreigners.

At $1.25 a dozen in 1961, many people could afford to buy a whole bushel. But Dad rarely bought more than two dozen because MM sometimes had an allergic reaction to them. We always supplemented our seafood meal with a huge fresh bluefish or some other catch, scaling and gutting the fish ourselves at home.

The other side of the Wharf called to us. Many Sunday afternoons Dad took us for a picnic at Hains Point, a mile-long peninsula that jutted out into the Potomac just across from where the SW seafood houses were located. MM and I rented bicycles and circled the point for hours while Dad read his *Washington Post* at the picnic table or took a nap in the grass.

Leaving the grounds of Hains Point with a rented bicycle was not allowed, but occasionally someone went beyond the boundaries, following the Potomac River to Georgetown. The big draw for weekend cyclists was the C&O Canal. You could ride the 100 miles from Georgetown to Cumberland and never leave the towpath. The ride was smooth and even with virtually no hills to climb. We never went beyond the canal's milepost at Glen Echo. This was our boundary. Fletcher's Boat House near Georgetown had its own bicycle rentals and even leased out canoes and rowboats. A bicycle all to yourself! Renting the bicycles was such a luxury since we had to share at St. Vincent's—about 20 girls to each bike.

We stood at the iron railing at the river's edge while Dad pointed out the landmarks on the shoreline—"There's the Wharf... the Yacht clubs and the Marina... the famous seafood restaurants... down a bit you see the Marine Barracks." Dad called the Marine Barracks "Eighth and I." And beyond what was visible was *Hall's on the River.* He claimed, "They have the best seafood in Washington."

He bragged that his boss Major Wills knew the inside scoop about plans for a boardwalk to be built from the Wharf up to the Marine Barracks. This gossip had come straight from the horse's mouth— from the D.C. Commissioner who lived down the street from Major on Ashmead Place. For years we waited to see this happen. We had been to Atlantic City and we envisioned a horse diving off a steel pier right into the Potomac. The boardwalk never materialized.

We were more enamored with the other side of the peninsula at Hains Point. It had very little "futuristic" promise because everything we loved was already right there. The water was choppier on that side. In the distance you could see trains passing over the tressle crossing into the Commonwealth of Virginia. There were planes taking off and landing at National Airport every several minutes. This hub was a mecca for escapism. This is where we did our dreaming.

Many children dream they can fly. In my dreams I escaped the home as I pushed myself off the second-floor porch at St. Vincent's, and then did a breast stroke to get to an altitude just above the trees.

I could get away from the kids at school who laughed at me and MM because we lived in "the home." My "flights" let me run away from the torment of not living in a normal home with my parents. My dreams always had a rainbow which I followed, flapping my arms wildly, always ending up at Hains Point.

On the way home from Hains Point, Dad would cross the bridge into Virginia and travel along the highway so that we could get the full view of the Washington skyline and Georgetown. Then he'd cross back over at the Chain Bridge into D.C. Crossing the Potomac River was always an adventure. While riding along the river on the Marshall Hall boat, one of the many outings for the girls of St. Vincent's, we conjured up great voyages in which we had been captured by pirates on the high seas.

During an outing in school to hear the National Symphony Orchestra, I was first introduced to the composer Smetana's musical masterpiece *The Moldau.* From then on, the muddy, murky Potomac became the beautiful Moldau River. I was carried away with the power of the strings of the violins and the pounding of the percussion. My over-active imagination brought me through the passages of *The Moldau* and simultaneosly carried me through the passages of my uneventful, colorless existence lived near the Potomac River. I loved the song "Old Man River" from *Showboat* but it was too depressing to embrace even for me. Life held so much drama for a St. Vincent adolescent.

We went with Dad when he picked up his friend Eduardo from Union Station. Eduardo rode the train from Baltimore. The station was dirty but it brimmed over with excitement. We went early and had breakfast at the newsstand. Dad got his shoes shined and told us the stories about the restaurant he owned and operated in Baltimore when he first got out of the Navy after World War I.

Outside we admired the huge marble building and walked around the Columbus statue in the middle of a huge fountain. I asked Dad if the statue was St. Christopher, the man who carried Jesus on his shoulders and was called the patron saint of travelers.

"I do not know that Christopher." Dad tried to educate me. "This statue is in honor of the Christopher who discovered America."

It still confused me. Why was this statue at the train station?

The streetcar stopped right in front of Union Station and Eduardo could have taken it home. But Dad said he had a lot of baggage.

Rita McAuliff lived at Sherwood Forest near Annapolis, Maryland during the summer. Sherwood took its theme from the Robin Hood adventures. Rita's home, a humble three-bedroom cottage amidst homes of every size in a private wooded development, was the most comfortable and welcoming home we'd been in. Built on the Severn River, the lazy sandy Sherwood Beach was diagonally across and just a short distance from the Naval Academy.

In the summer, Rita took groups of girls from St. Vincent's for the weekend. She had gone to school at St. Rose's in Washington and was the stamina behind the Ladies Auxiliary at St. Vincent's. She shared her home. She spoiled us. She let us dabble in her kitchen, something we could never do at St. Vincent's. She took us to Mass on Sunday at the community center which was said by a visiting priest from Annapolis.

Rita even loaned us her father, "Mister Mac," who took us crabbing on the pier and fishing in his small motorboat. Mister Mac even smoothed down Rita's feathers when she found out we had spent an afternoon with some boys from Sherwood beyond the geographic boundaries she set for us.

Rita also shared her home with some of the Sisters and other friends. She provided us with relaxing, carefree days. A trip to Rita's place at Sherwood was more than an outing. It was a true "journey" from our everyday world. Rita accepted us as though we were her kids. Rita loved us. She always included us for the jaunt.

Beyond the Gates

When we were teenagers, leaving the gates at St. Vincent's was like taking a quick walk between childhood and the future. You were used to your familiar life at St. Vincent's. It was safe, stable, and predictable, the way childhood should be. Inside the walls of our home, we learned to cope with the underlying hurt that persisted from the many disappointments in our lives. There was lots of support and understanding from peers. We fared well even without the help of professional counseling although counseling was made available to some girls.

When we left the gates each day we could not rely on the outside world to be the same sheltered harbor of safety. We were never really prepared for the new brand of pain that was to come.

My Aunt Clara said my mother was working at People's Drug Store at Thomas Circle. I cut cheerleading practice several times to go see her there, about a 15-minute walk from school, and finally caught up with her one afternoon. She worked behind the soda fountain. I sat at the counter, so happy to see her. She didn't tell me where she was living but she bought me a cherry Coke and a beef burger.

I was ready to pour my heart out to her—I had made the cheerleading squad. I missed her. Sister was going to let me get my ears pierced. MM was having a baby so she would be having her first grandchild. I wanted her number so I could call her sometime. There was so much to say to her. She flinched when her admirers at work heard me call her "Mom," preferring her nickname, "Tina." Her sisters and her close friends called her "Teenie."

In between taking care of her customers and wiping off the counter, she told me the latest gossip about her sister. Then, taking a 10-minute cigarette break in one of the booths, she puffed a Kool and gave me the low down on her new man, a guy named Brooks. And oh, did I know that, "Mr. Thomas from H Street was arrested again for drunk driving?"

I went to visit Mom again in a few weeks, but the manager told me she quit and moved to Norfolk. He didn't have an address for her.

Walking to the Franciscan Monastery was an enjoyable jaunt, which we took many times when the weather was nice. It was a chance for reflection and meditation. Sitting quietly in the beautiful church, gazing at the life-size statue of the Hanging Christ with His Blessed Mother, or touring the Catacombs gave us time to put things in better perspective.

Going beyond the gates could sometimes have unusual consequences. Sometimes girls would travel north or east to distant parts of Maryland, and south. The "Pó-to-mack," as it was referred to lovingly by our school and home Sisters, seemed to the be the invisible fence that kept us grounded. To travel beyond the canal and to traverse the bridges that crossed into Virginia was definitely breaking out of our ordinary turf in Northeast Washington, D.C. and the immediate10-mile radius of our little world.

Stella Hill was ready to enter her sophomore year at Notre Dame Academy. Her father's work took him away from the D.C. area. He wrote to her periodically, always promising that he would soon have enough money saved up to take her out of St. Vincent's for good. One Friday afternoon he arrived and planned to take Stella for the weekend. He was greeted by Sister Elizabeth who managed the office. She told him that he would have to get permission from Stella's social worker before she could go for the whole weekend. Mr. Hill was not very happy about this, but agreed to take Stella out just for dinner that night.

During the meal, and after a few drinks, Mr. Hill became increasingly upset that anyone would try to tell him that he could not take his daughter for an overnight visit without permission. After dinner, Mr. Hill had a taxi take them to the airport. Stella left the security and stability of "life behind the gates" for the chaos and uncertainty of life in New York City with a well meaning but troubled and alcoholic father. Within a few years she was married with two children.

Several times in Sister Bernard's high school group, Jamie, several other girls, and I were invited to have breakfast with Miss Nally. We had seen her around many times. She was a tall woman, always dressed in a business suit and a hat. Miss Nally was in charge of the Ladies' Auxiliary.

She seemed to enjoy sharing meals with us at the Hot Shoppes on Rhode Island Avenue, the one near the Village Theatre, and she always paid special attention to our conversation. On one occasion we were discussing how the Cuban girls in our group made their special coffee—café con leche. She found it interesting and viewed it as a unique piece of their culture. Miss Nally always made a point of saving the creamers and sugar packets for us to bring back to the Cuban girls, and was not even embarrassed to ask the waiter to pack us some extra packets, "for the girls we left at the Home."

This comment got attention and pulled the waiters in for questions about St. Vincent's. Miss Nally, an attorney, and the epitome of the "self-actualized" individual in a psychological hierarchy of needs, never flinched when the waiters probed for more details. She had a very matter-of-fact attitude about St. Vincent's being an orphanage but rather spoke of it as though it were a fine European boarding school or a finishing school. As she paid the bill and pulled on her white gloves, nose held respectably high, she commented that, incidentally, "These girls are definitely not orphans."

Miss Nally was a positive role model for achievement and for reaching spiritual fulfillment. And because of my observations on the trips with her to the Hot Shoppes, she launched my hobby as a scavenger of condiment packets and other goodies from restaurants!

The trip to the Naval Gun Factory always kicked off the Christmas season and lead to other outings, such as good Catholic families coming to take two or three girls out for a meal in their homes, or local school groups coming to entertain. The high school girls enjoyed another tradition—a "Progressive" Christmas Party—courtesy of Rita McAuliff and some of the other volunteers. The ever so patient volunteers logged in a gazillion miles on the old station wagon, going from appetizers at Pat Foley's in Annapolis, to dinner at Catherine Jarboe's in Falls Church. We ended the progressive party at Mary Lou Deaver's in Hillcrest Heights for dessert and to hear Christmas carols played on the organ in her living room. Her house was filled with about half a dozen sons. The order for the house visitations varied every year.

Another trip especially for growing teenage girls was a trip with Rita McAuliff to Waldorf, Maryland, to go dancing at a club, something very unique from our usual routine.

The Shady Grove Music Festival had its own ampitheater near Gaithersburg, Maryland, about a 45-minute ride from St. Vincent's. We saw the musical *Oliver*, and of course we identified strongly with the shabby, poor little urchins holding out their bowls singing the song about "food, glorious food." We also saw *Showboat* which had the wonderful song "Old Man River."

On a summer trip to tour the FBI building downtown, Jamie was thrown from the seat of a D.C. Transit charter bus. She was not even aware that she had received a big gash on her forehead when she was forced into a pole, then to the floor of the bus, and needed medical attention.

Jamie insisted she was fine but finally consented to have someone look at her. An ambulance was called. She was transported to Providence Hospital. The rest of us went on to the FBI.

We brought her back the target practice sheet. She was fine when we got back. You might say that the bump on her head put a few more brain cells in place, for Jamie, who was constantly told she was not bright, proved over the years to be one of the most brilliant students of our lot. She received a financial settlement from D.C. Transit, very small, which funded the down payment for her first car, a 1957 red and white Chevy station wagon. She was also the first among our peers to drive.

That same year Julie, Jamie and I enjoyed the most exciting trip of our lives—we went to New York City. The Sisters made this trip often and usually stayed several days. This time the trip was just to go up and back quickly.

Bill Marean drove several of the Sisters and the three of us in the station wagon for the 200-mile trip. The Sisters were still not allowed to drive a vehicle. Bill taught Jamie a lot about driving and Jamie was the first of our group to get a drivers' license.

Up to that point in my young life, Atlantic City, New Jersey was as far as I had ever been. Julie and Jamie had only gone about as far as Baltimore, Maryland or to Rita McAuliff's beach cottage at Sherwood Forest near Annapolis, Maryland.

The Sisters had business to attend to in Jamaica Plains. We thought it was another home run by the Daughters of Charity. Sister Bernard wanted us to enjoy ourselves and had taken money from each of our books for us to go shopping in Manhattan. Bill Marean dropped us off at a newsstand near Macy's, and made plans to return to the same spot in two hours.

Two hours. We had two glorious hours to shop so we headed straight for Macy's. It was every bit as exciting as the scenes from the movie *Miracle on 34th Street*. A quick look on the first floor showed us that the prices were more than we had expected. The basement beckoned us.

We were determined to follow the tradition of rummaging. We rummaged through piles and piles of clearance clothing, reaching to the bottom of each display table for bargains, till we found something we wanted. We each bought blouses and then ate at a Horn & Horn Automat, the most gigantic vending-machine restaurant we had ever seen. We got back to the pickup point just in time.

We had bragging rights and exercised them when we returned home. After all, we had spent a wonderful day in New York City!

November 22, 1963 was just another ordinary day at St. Patrick's Academy, until we heard the horrible words over the loudspeaker at the end of our last class of the day, "President Kennedy has been shot. There is no further information." We were asked to resume classes as usual but almost everyone at school, frightened and in shock, left for home.

Some of us made our way to the only television in school, which was across from the business office on the first floor. Many of the Sisters joined us as we sat glued to the TV. We needed to have the horrific news verified by the constant repetition of the news on each channel. President Kennedy had been shot. Then the news confirmed that President Kennedy was dead! At our usual dismissal time, 2:30 p.m., our school was immediately like a ghost town. The basketball team came into the auditorium, standing around with the cheerleaders, retelling the horrible events of this day.

Then we slowly trickled out of the building, under a cloud of doom, making our way home. The City was paralyzed. People walked around F Street in a daze, bumping into one another, hugging one another, crying, the cold air not affecting anyone.

Jamie and the Frank sisters felt compelled to visit the Capitol when President Kennedy's body was laid there to rest. It was very late in the evening. They wanted to go to St. Matthew's Cathedral the next morning for the funeral service. Knowing they could never get in the doors, they visited very early in the morning and said their farewells.

The Potomac River once again girdled us in; none of us ventured beyond the bridges into Virginia. We watched all of the events on TV that occurred after President Kennedy's body had been brought home, back to DC—from having been lain in State at the Capitol for the throngs of people who paid their last respects to the Commander in Chief to the funeral with unprecedented attendance at St. Matthews, and on to the last procession from the Cathedral to the burial grounds at Arlington National Cemetary.

Many of those who witnessed the somber march first hand of the horse-drawn casson that carried his body toward Arlington stopped themselves at the Memorial Bridge. They followed with their eyes, and grieved with their breaking hearts as their President passed over the river.

The Christmas season came that year but without a lot of notice by Washingtonians. The City was in a slump. Downtown remained sober for months.

Friends for a Lifetime

"Birds of a Feather Flock Together!" Sister Bernard said this often about me and Jamie. It was true. We have been friends for a lifetime. Our bonding took place immediately when we met in Sister Bernard's high school group after I returned to St. Vincent's in the summer of 1961.

Jamie came to St. Vincent's at the beginning of eighth grade and remained there through high school. She was not really impressed with my former social life. Being on the Milt Grant Show to her was important because it gave me a social outlet. But she was not envious of the short-term "fame" I had. After all, it was just a dance show. Jamie could get more impressed by music—the kind you perform yourself. She played clarinet. She hated "flashy, frilly" things and swears that "patent leather shoes *do* shine up!" in response to the silly question asked of people who attended Catholic schools as kids.

In her high school days, Jamie involved herself in a variety of activities. Her favorite past-times proved to be far more noble pursuits than the usual teenage interests like the rest of her colleagues in our high school group. She joined the Sodality of the Miraculous Medal. One weekend she attended a huge gathering which was held at St. Joseph's Home for Boys. There were teens from all over the United States.

Sister Bernard went on retreat for a few days and left Jamie in charge of the candy shoppe. That responsibility she assumed involved a lot of dealings with the kitchen, and a great deal of time interacting with the cook, Miss Emma. She soon realized how less-than-jolly Miss Betty could get when someone tampered with her kitchen for any reason—sometimes even "barking" at sweet Miss Emma if things were moved around without her say-so.

The usual supply of ice cream did not get delivered for the candy shop so Jamie came up with a creative solution for capturing the "ice cream" monies. There was an overstock of chocolate milk. Miss Emma let her freeze it and sell it in the candy shoppe as a new five-cent "icey chocolate" snack.

Sister Elizabeth, who managed the office and most of the fiscal matters at St. Vincent's discovered Jamie was selling the chocolate milk which we had turned into an ice cream substitute. She told her the milk had a clear message right on the packaging. In big bold letters it stated it was "issued for non-profits—not to be resold" Sister stopped the "illegal" sales and turned in the bountiful profit Jamie had gleaned, placing the money in the petty cash fund.

Sister Elizabeth, appreciating Jamie's entrepreneurial spirit, fine tuned her interest in accounting. Jamie worked with Sister on the books in the office and sharpened her skills, carefully heeding Sister's words, "It's all possible when you do things legally."

One year Jamie was chosen to be the "May Queen." She was to encircle the head of the statue of the Blessed Virgin Mary with a crown made from fresh May flower blossoms. The statue was in the front of the building. Being selected as May Queen was quite an honor. There would be other girls from other groups that would "crown" other statues of Mary, three of them throughout the property, but the crowning of the statute in the front, flanked by the white dogwood trees and roses, was the highlight of the May Procession and something to remember always.

Jamie wanted to do a good job, as she always did with each of the assignments she was given. She scoped out the route that the May Procession would take in advance, noticing that the birds of Edgewood Street had already "crowned" the statues to be crowned. The birds always dressed them too, with a crusty, familiar textured material. As a matter, of fact, to Jamie the statues were rather over-loaded with the white runny "birdie trim" most of the time. But when she boldly got some paint to give the statues new life, she noticed how strangely plain they appeared, almost stripped down to the plaster. Nevertheless, she and several other girls painted the statues a clean white color. Jamie learned that Sister had recently cleaned the statues to get them ready for the May Procession, using a power wash or sand blasting technique. You would expect the incident would bring on a hearty laugh and one could say that it was an example of "two great minds working in the same direction!" Needless to say, that's not exactly what Sister said.

Bill Marean, who drove the Sisters to their appointments, had a number of odds-n-end jobs around St. Vincent's. He asked Jamie to share in one of the jobs, turning on the sprinklers every night. She was to turn them off several hours later. In the wintertime she had inherited the thankless job of shaking off the huge fir trees burdened down with the weight of the new-fallen snow. Throughout the 19-acres and the interior of the St. Vincent facility, Jamie was delegated jobs that required a logical mind, self-reliancy and a good sense of judgement. She had the keys to the swimming pool, the candy shoppe and any other doors or locks that could keep nosy little girls out of places they did not belong. She also worked for Monsignor Gallagher, who had private residential quarters on the first floor, bringing him meals and doing minor housekeeping chores. She enjoyed his stories about driving to Catholic Charities where he was Director for many years.

Jamie was asked to help out with taking care of the little ones in both Sister Anna and Sister Alma's groups. She was only in eighth grade herself. She took this responsibility on willingly and proved to be a great asset to both the Sisters when they needed to leave her in charge of the little girls in their absence.

Jamie visited Sister Monica's laundry quite often. This was the facility for laundering the Sister's habits. It was one of the few areas for which Jamie had no direct responsibility, but was fascinated with the starching operation of the cornettes and collars, nonetheless.

Just outside of the laundry were the offices for the social workers.

Not especially fond of the social workers' visits. The social workers came, they interviewed us and they left. But no changes were made—good or bad. And we still remained at St. Vincent's for lack of better alternatives. I personally thought the former usage of these rooms was better—as arts and crafts rooms.

Selma Frank, who worked at St. Vincent's, was employed as a seamstress. Her three daughters, Terrie, Ginger and Melanie, were also pals of Jamie. Selma was a close runner-up to Jamie in terms of how many duties they each had. The family lived in Maryland and the Frank sisters, very close in age to each other and to Jamie, went to suburban Catholic schools. During the summer months the girls would accompany Mrs. Frank to work for the day. The Frank family accepted Jamie completely, including her in many weekends and holidays at their home in Maryland.

Jamie suffered from a very low self-esteem. Perhaps it was because she had been told many times in her lifetime that she was not very worthy of much attention and that she was "not very bright." Nothing could be farther from the truth. She was the most intelligent, shrewd, incisive and politically-astute resident that St. Vincent's ever turned out. Her actions reflected her steady thinking on a much higher plane than the rest of us. She had great ambitions for herself personally. But they were overshadowed by her concern for social justice and her sensitivity to not hurt anyone.

She applied for and got into St. Anthony's High School in Brookland, preferring to stay in the one-mile neighborhood rather than attending Immaculate Conception which was several miles from St. Vincent's. St. Anthony's had another plus—it was "co-educational," the only Catholic high school in the area. We thought that Bishop O'Connell High School in Virginia was co-ed, but Jamie understood the difference between "co-educational"—for male and female students in the same classrooms and "co-institutional"—for male and female students with classes conducted separately. Jamie was always very judicious in matters that required such fine tuning.

¡Cuba, Sí. Yanqui, No!

"Oyeme, Mariana, yo compré una vestida."

"Un vestido, estúpida.

"Bueno, un vestido."

"Tu tienes que practicar."

"C'mon, I thought I was doing great for a beginner."

"But Juani, es-still you make mistakes on feminine or masculine words. And you cannot pronounce the 'r' or the double 'rr,' chinita! You sound like a Chinese girl! The Chinese always es-speak a funny 'r' in es-Spanish. They cannot roll the 'r.' It comes out like the 'l' or something."

"Es-speak es-Spanish?" I teased back using my best accent. She was now losing her patience helping me with my Spanish. Mariana was in the other high school group and I did not want to always feel like I was bugging her too much.

"Chinita, chinita, toca la malaca." She pulled my hair and did a little dance as she teased me and went to visit her country mates in the next room.

During the few years that I was gone from St. Vincent's, living in various homes and situations, St. Vincent's had opened its doors to more than 15 Cuban girls through a special program administered by Catholic Charities. In the middle of the night in the Spring 1961, the Cuban girls came to live at St. Vincent's.

The Cuban girls had surnames that resounded off the tongue so melodically, like reading a listing from a society column or the 1958 *Who's Who in old Havana and Santiago de Cuba*: García, Velasquez, Mendez, Suarez, Rodriguez, Lopez, Ortega, Ordoñez, Mendoza.

Fidel Castro was in power. Loved and hated, the brilliant orator, who holds a law degree, took control of Cuba in 1959, declaring himself prime minister, after an "age of decadence" fluorished under two-term President Fulgencio Batista's rule. During Batista's era, the elite enjoyed a grand lifestyle and the majority of the rural population suffered great poverty. The year 1959 is modern Cuba's "year zero."

The Revolution brought radical changes to Cuba. Religious affiliation was considered "anti-revolutionary." Anyone seen as non-supportive of the government was deemed socially unacceptable; many of these non-conformists were jailed. Trade unions were split up. The media was under the absolute control of the government. Homosexuals were imprisoned in labor camps.

What we learned from the Cubans who took refuge just 90 miles from their homeland, and later in Washington, D.C. at St. Vincent's, was more realistic and familiar to us. Families were separated. Personal property was confiscated. The arts were virtually dead. And "Big Brother" was always watching you.

The office of Catholic Charities worked diligently to get these girls into good homes or institutions, sending them, from the time they arrived in Miami, to locations throughout the country.

"Sea stair, can we get some more Sweeetheart soap?" Melinda asked Sister Bernard. The Americans would roll their eyes in disbelief, wondering how Sister could fall for the sweet-talking of the Cubans whenever they wanted some special favors. They were always making demands of Sister, but of course always very diplomatically. And they always got what they asked for.

The dormitory situation was a lot different at St. Vincent's once you hit high school. They tried very hard to place no more than five or six girls to a room to make the dormitories seem a little more comfortable and homey.

In reorganizing rooms and roommates, I supposed someone in the office, not familiar with every single girl, looked at my Spanish surname—*Mondoñedo*—and assumed I must be Cuban too. After a lot of trial and error in organizing the dormitories, I was placed in a small dorm with my friend Julie and two Cuban girls. And I don't know why but they threw into the dorm an all-American redhead—Julie Camden. Maybe it was the I-love-Lucy thing, what with Lucille Ball, the redhead, being married to Desi Arnaz from Cuba. Or maybe because Julie claimed to know a little Spanish and might communicate better. Who knows.

So it was sink or swim in our dorm. Learn a little Spanish to survive or be left out. Julie was called *la peliroja* because of the color of her hair. I was Juanita, *la Chinita*, or just plain *Juani*. Jamie spent lots of time with Julie and I and the Cubans whenever she could. She also knew a little Spanish.

The Cubans used makeup when they dressed to go somewhere but usually were clean-faced otherwise. They enjoyed watching Julie go from "ordinary" to "spectacular" by the use of makeup. It may have taken her an hour to apply her makeup and do her hair but we were sure she could have passed for an Ann-Margaret double when she was dressed to go out.

Being placed in the Cuban dorm and being urged to learn Spanish was by far the most exciting time of my life up to that point. The Cubans spoke English very well, most of them having been educated in American Dominican schools in Cuba. But they naturally broke into Spanish amongst themselves. Julie and I were mesmerized by the sound of the language, their pierced earrings, their "real" gold jewelry and their music. We parroted their mannerisms, we were excited the first time they experienced snow and listened in awe to their stories of their coming-out parties in pre-Castro times in Cuba. We shopped for gold bracelets like theirs and we merengued along with them whenever we heard a Cugat rhythm.

We even learned to pronounce "Xavier" correctly. I bought a high school Spanish grammar book, *El Camino Real*, and studied Spanish, spending hours and hours, attempting to pronounce popular tongue twisters, *trabalenguas* like "...erre con erre, cigarro, erre con erre, barril.." and learning to roll my Rs in words like *burro* and *Ricky Ricardo*, just for their approval.

Meanwhile, our fellow American orphans were finding fault with them. The Cubans were spoiled. The Cubans were rude. The Cubans always broke into Spanish whenever they did not want us to know what was going on. And they were perpetually wrapping *Sea Stair* around their little Cuban fingers..

It did not seem to matter to the other American girls that most of the Cubans were at least three or four years older than the rest of us, some in college, and that they had lived quite different lives and were trying to adjust to an atypical lifestyle at St. Vincent's.

They had very different views on almost any topic we could pick. National politics meant absolutely nothing to them. They were always tuning in to radio or television announcements that might carry international news. When would Castro leave Cuba? Details about rumors of threats on Castro's life. What was the United States doing to get Castro out of power? These are the topics that interested them.

Perhaps we should have been resentful for the bigger "perks" the Cubans seemed to get. Many of them attended Catholic University tuition free, something the American girls could only dream of doing. But in view of all they had lost by fleeing from their country, going to college for free seemed like a small gift.

My dear friend, Mary Elisabeth Holmes, who was in the younger groups with me when I lived at St. Vincent's in the 1950s was placed in Sister Catherine's high school group. It was just on the other side of the chapel. I missed her and rarely saw her because she went to Immaculate Conception Academy and took a different bus to get there. But there were some times when the entire house got together or "Lizzie" and I could reminisce about the "old days," the 1950s at St. Vincent's, and create additional chronicles of our friendship.

Francy Becker was in the other high school group too and she used to help Lavinia with her English. One night Francy and Lavinia were sitting out on the fire escape porch. Mary Elisabeth was inside. When they came in, Lavinia said, "Good night, Mary Elizabeth and God bless you, you son of a bitch." They always said, "Good night and God bless you." But she had just innocently learned the latter part from Frances.

The cultural exchange was not one-sided, though. We all learned to flick our forefingers in that distinctive Cuban style and shout, "Ay, carájo" in place of the usual expression for "damn" or to express disgust.

A couple of the Cuban girls attended Catholic University, just a one-mile walk from St. Vincent's. Their political science classes must have included lively discussions on Cuba and Communism. They all seemed to have a wide network of fellow Cubans in Washington, D.C., always ready to welcome others who had just escaped from Cuba. They were referred to as "exiles" or "refugees" but to call them that would have been as politically incorrect as calling the American girls at St. Vincent's "orphans."

Our Superior at the time, Sister Genevieve allowed the Cubans to have a big party one evening, inviting a few outsiders, including some of the Cuban boys who lived at St. Joseph's Home in Northeast. The music and the food were wonderful and we got to meet the most handsome boy named Miguel. To the Cubans, Miguel was just a little kid; to the Americans he was perfect—tall, dark, handsome, and he had a sexy Desi Arnaz accent.

Getting ready for this big party was exciting, almost what we had envisioned our Cuban roommates' 15th Birthday or "Coming-out" Party would have been in pre-Castro Cuba. The dormitory was a wreck with the makeup strewn everywhere and the room exuded scents of exotic perfumes. Everyone's constant change of clothing added to the hectic mood. It looked like an MGM production with the Cuban girls starring in roles fit for Carmen Miranda.

The Cubans loved to dance. There was always wonderful music playing in our high school group. When the full contingent of Cubans got together, it was like a fiesta. Rosi Juarez played the guitar. The Americans' favorite tune was the Mexican song "Cielito Lindo," because we could sing along with lyrics that were easy to learn.

But a beloved Cuban guajira ballad, a peasant song, was *Guantanamera*. The song was written by the most famous guajira ballad songwriter, Joseito Fernandez, who used the words from the famous poem "Un Hombre Sincero," by the well-loved Cuban poet and hero, Jose Martí—"Yo soy un hombre sincero, de donde crece la palma."

From the folk-song era of the 1960s, another haunting melody came out, that seemed to make the Cubans so sad. I finally cried in sympathy when my pigeon Spanish improved and I understood the words that went "...cuando iré de Cuba, deje mi alma, mi corazón."

In my sophomore and junior years I had a great friend who lived at St. Vincent's who was like a big sister to me—Ana Peregrin. Ana attended St. Patrick's Academy with me and Marina Bianca, another very sweet and very attractive young lady who was from Camaguey, Cuba. We all took the same bus, (guagua) together to get to St. Patrick's.

Marina, Ana and the other Cuban girls told us stories about their pre-American days and their "coming out" parties. Marina longed to be back in Camaguey in the countryside she missed so much. Rural Camaguey, called the "heart of the heartland," is the home of the Cuban peasant—el guajiro.

Ana, taller than I by three or four inches, was a little on the chunky side, always trying to diet. She dressed impeccably and told me that one day I, Juani to her, would learn that men like women with hips. She also advised me not to soak in the bathtub that had been freshly scrubbed with Dutch Cleanser, something that had to be done by each girl between each bath, warning that "this too," if I ever wanted children, is "something you will discover when you mature."

Julie from our dorm at St. Vincent's bought a new product—Tausaway—a sort of rubber plug-like cup that acted as a tampon. Julie was the ultimate consumer. She would not go anywhere without at least an hour's prep time to apply makeup and dressing "to kill" or at least getting admiring attention. Amazed by her avant garde acquisitions, we were not surprised to have Julie slam the bathroom door in our faces on the day she inserted the plug into herself. It had only taken Julie 20 minutes and as she emerged victoriously from the toilet stall and left the bathroom, Ana was adamant that Julie would never bear children. What did I know? At age 16, I didn't have the nerve to even use a tampon.

Ana didn't have to say much to convince me not to use the plug. I had better things to do with the little bit of money I had on my book. Like buying cheap gold bracelets from the Treasure Trove on F Street thinking they would not turn my arm green or thinking they could compete with Ana's solid gold bracelet she received as a little girl. Per the custom, she received another bracelet each year. I also tried to impress a friend of Ana's who worked at Garfinkel's by making a whopping $10 purchase—a small fortune for me in those days.

At school I was jealous of Ana and Marina because my favorite nun, typing and shorthand teacher and basketball coach—Sister Clarence Marie spoke excellent Spanish and had a wonderful relationship with them. For a talent show Ana and Marina dressed up Caribbean style and danced a cha-cha. I wanted so much to be included but Sister said she wanted to let them show off a bit of their culture for the whole school. I was green with envy. I guess it was like "idol worship." Ana was like a big sister to me, and I wanted to be around her all of the time.

When Ana and Marina graduated from St. Patrick's Academy they went to live with friends in the D.C. area. I miss them.

A head covering for women was mandatory in Church. Ana and the other Cuban girls wore some of the most beautiful lace *mantillas*, short veils, in Chapel instead of hats or the tiny little lace coverlet, about six inches in diameter, that we were used to wearing on our heads. The familiar little veil was a step up from wearing a "beanie" at school in the younger grades. This was secured by bobby pins on both sides of the little cap that sat on the top of your head.

If any one of us made the big investment to buy a longer, triangle-shaped *mantilla*, the Cubans would yank it off the girl's head and remind her not to wear it "upside down." This was incorrect.

"The sides should drape over your shoulders; the rounded edge should be placed over the front of your head." That's what they told us. We must have appeared very ignorant, uncoordinated and extremely unsophisticated to them.

The Cubans observed the American custom of getting dressed up in your "Sunday best" for Mass. They were used to dressing *up* for parties but dressing *down* for Mass. They said it was done to avoid drawing attention to yourself in Church. It made sense to us, but Sister did not go for the new cultural custom they were trying to introduce.

Some days the tension felt like warfare. There was a lot of miscommunication because of English. Many of the battles were cultural in nature. Most were turf issues. In retrospect, the battles were very minor.

The chapel seem to be the great equalizer for the Americans and the Cubans. Since the Mass was said in Latin, the issue of Spanish vs. English dissipated.

All of the Cubans really did know how to capitalize on Sister Bernard's weaknesses, the primary one being Sister's love of the Kennedy family. Of course the Cubans loved his foreign policy to open the doors of the U.S. to Cuban refugees. Charismatic John Kennedy was extremely handsome and the Kennedy children were adorable. And of course the beautiful Jackie Kennedy, wowed any impressionable, romantic young woman—Cubana or Yanqui—with her beautiful fashions and style and she even spoke Spanish.

For Sister, the sun rose and set because of the Kennedy family. There were photographs of the Kennedy family throughout the living room areas. Sister referred to President Kennedy as though she were speaking of a Prince. But she referred to the First Lady and their children by first names, as though they lived on another floor at St. Vincent's. The Kennedys were simply a cut above normal people yet she called Jackie by name as though she were our big sister or aunt. The Kennedys triumphs and tragedies were Sister Bernard's personal blessings or crosses to bear.

A very difficult period of time for the Cubans were the dark days of the Cuban Missile Crisis. The United States saw Castro as a threat to national security. Strange events took place, leading up to the Cuban Missile Crisis, beginning in 1960, when Fidel Castro delivered his first speech to the United Nations, and at that same time met Soviet premier, Nikita Krushchev and, while in New York, radical American Black Power leader Malcom X.

Every day there was news about Cuba. The severance of diplomatic ties in 1961, with 11 American diplomats thrown out of Cuba. The United States' economic embargo of Cuba. Latin America cut trade and diplomatic ties with Cuba. The attempt to instigate a coup again Castro in 1961 in the Bay of Pigs. The humiliating trade of prisoners for $50 million worth of medicine to Cuba. Castro's allegiance to Marxism and U.S.S.R.'s subsequent economic aid and nuclear missiles for Cuba. Finally in 1962 the Soviet Union and the United States clashed head to head with the reality of nuclear war.

In the weeks during the Cuban Missile Crisis, disaster plans were made in our schools. What if the tension were to escalate into an out-and-out war? What would become of us if someone in Moscow got nervous and fired a missile? We knew very well that we Washingtonians were the target and we would not survive an attack. Most schools preferred to have the children sent home rather then kept in classrooms. But most schools did not have safe areas for the children. St. Patrick's had semi-underground areas that were more than adequate as fall-out shelters. With the impending catastrophe looming over us in those days, we assumed we would use the fall-out shelters in the event of an attack on Washington. At home at St. Vincent's, our unrehearsed plan was to climb under a bed and hope for the best.

These were wooly times. The future looked unclear to us. Every evening we would sit around the television set to take in the latest news about what our President and the other world leaders were doing to relieve the international tension in those final difficult days. Suddenly the world seemed smaller. The world map displayed on the tube looked like a giant interactive chess set with each of the players bluffing, plotting their next move. There was so much at stake and we all rooted and prayed for President John Kennedy's threat to pay off.

In that short span of time we grew up a little and learned a lot more about life. Crying, praying, bonding. We gained a new respect for one another. The labels we placed on one another were erased for a period of time. The American girls could finally have compassion for the Cubans' tragic loss of family, country and all that they held dear. The Cuban girls could appreciate the might of America, the glory of the freedom and the fleeting quality of life. In our little world at St. Vincent's, the slogan "¡Cuba si; Yanquis, no!" became words for the history books only.

Noxema Covers Scars

You can take the girl out of the orphanage but you can't take the orphanage out of the girl! There are things that remain with us from our experiences at St. Vincent's. We can never forget from where we came. Although most of our experiences were positive and redeeming, there are so many invisible wounds that bandages cannot heal from our trauma.

Julie Camden knew the beauty of makeup. She never went out the door without her "full face"—foundation, eyeliner, eyebrow pencil, mascara, rouge, lipstick and dusting powder. She relied on the Cover Girl Company to transform her sweet, healthy, freckled face into moviestar-quality beauty. And she performed this miraculous ritual before our very eyes in the lavatory at St. Vincent's. Julie was in fact the "Mistress of Cover and Conceal."

Linda Hawkins came back, depressed, from a visit with her father and brothers after a holiday weekend. I saw her in the lavatory, staring at herself in the mirror. She had a 3-inch gash on her face, which she had been trying to cover up with Noxzema. After spending half an hour with her, coaxing her to tell me what happened, she admitted one of her brothers cut her face after a big argument.

It was not the first time. Linda had incidents like this all of the time. Her brothers were left alone most of the time because their father had to work. They lived in a rough neighborhood off Benning Road in D.C. And simply put, her brothers were mean. After that visit, she decided she would not spend the weekend with her family any more.

Linda Johnson, whose parents were separated, used to go home with him once a month to his apartment in Arlington, Virginia. I never heard anything about her mother. She confided that they slept in the same bed, because he didn't have a bed for her, and "he treats me like his wife." Linda never explained what she meant by that. He was old, very old. I had some romantic notions that, just like my father, Mr. Johnson let her decorate the apartment and cook a meal for him. Surely this is what she meant. This is what makes a young girl happy.

Naïve? Most of us were. There were rumors that girls in our high school group were "queer" and that they were caught fondling one another and "making out" under the steps in the basement. This was never proven. We tried our best to stay away from these girls whenever possible just in case the story was true.

Marian Johns, a girl just 13 years old, went home for good—left St. Vincent's in a big hurry. No one got a goodbye from her. She went out to school one day and did not come back in the afternoon. No one even knew where she went. The rumor was that she got pregnant by a St. Joseph boy. Amazing, could it have been true? St. Joseph's Home for Boys in Northeast D.C. only went up to the eighth grade so the boy could not have been more than 13 or 14. However, we were convinced this rumor was true, because we witnessed Marian flirting with a visiting priest, and unbuttoning her shirt in front of the religious Brothers, volunteers who used to help us with homework and play outdoor games with us in the Grove after school. She had a history of boldly teasing men and boys and we didn't trust her.

Sexual contact was taboo. But the same rules that applied in any Catholic High School in the 1960s applied at St. Vincent's and then some. So this was not some cruel punishment. It was just the typical sexual repression of the 1960s.

But any physical contact was frowned upon. In all of my years at St. Vincent's I do not remember once being hugged or held by the

Sisters. Being "touchy-feely" was not the custom. It was perfectly acceptable to hug your siblings. Many of us became very clingy with our sisters. But hugging another girl was not acceptable. There was just some unwritten rule that tabooed displays of physical affection.

This was experienced by Peggy O'Reilly, one of the high girls, who had a great personal attachment to Sister Mary. One of her parents was an alcoholic; the other was involved in a new romantic relationship. Neither parent had the time nor the living space for her. Had it not been for her teacher at school recommending that she go to St. Vincent's to live, Peggy would have been homeless and ultimately in serious trouble, living on the streets of Southwest Washington, D.C.

Sister Mary was the first person in her lifetime that Peggy had learned to trust. Peggy could hardly believe in Sister's sincerity and her geuine kindness toward her. It was so new for her.

A very short time later this Sister was to be transferred to another mission. She wanted so much to hug her, to wish her well, to tell her goodbye, to thank her for all she had done for her. In reality, she wanted to cling to her like an infant holding onto its mother. But it just was not the custom to be physically demonstrative with anyone, especially the Sisters. Although we viewed the Sisters as our mothers, there was always the respect and distance maintained like that of teacher-student. Peggy had to restrict any physical contact with Sister.

Peggy saw her her only opportunity to be close to Sister would be in the chapel. It was the morning Sister was to leave St. Vincent's. Sister was sitting in the pew across from Peggy. After Mass was over, Peggy moved out to the aisle and genuflected next to Sister, kneeling down with her face as acceptably close to Sister's face as she could possibly get.

She stiffled her emotions. She held back the tears. Despite the lack of physical affection that we craved so much, we knew we were loved.

"God bless you, Sister," was all Peggy could say.

During these years life became more and more difficult. When we were in grade school we faced separation issues, separation from our families. We always felt cheated. We felt that since our home environment was institutional, not "normal," that we were therefore not normal.

Later, material things seemed important and we wished for things. Our own room, our own bike, our own record player.

But as we entered the teenage years, the typical problems experienced by most adolescents were compounded because we lived at St. Vincent's. We were growing up. Our problems got bigger and more complex.

The Sisters were our mentors, and they instilled in us deep spiritual values. But we needed honest-to-goodness, real flesh and blood role models. We wanted what we could not have. We wanted the intimacy of a family. And we needed guidance from our parents. And on a very practical side, we began to think about what we were going to do after high school graduation, which realistically meant, "What will we do when we no longer live at St. Vincent's?"

Unendingly, we tried to understand the issues, the primary reasons we were placed at St. Vincent's—death, divorce and alcoholism, abandonment. Many of us had spent all of our childhood at St. Vincent's and we wanted some resolution to those original problems.

Some of us continued to experience negative feelings about our self-worth. Academically we understood that death, divorce and other problems prevented us from being at home with our families. But as teenage girls, our emotions took over our rational thinking and we asked the same questions. "Why can't I have what everyone else has? Why did my parents separate (divorce or die)? Why do people stigmatize me for the actions of my parents?"

The scars of these conditions remained with us. We reacted negatively whenever we heard a phrase like "She came from a broken home," or the like. There would always remain a little bit of the rejected orphan in each of us.

The serenity prayer became a great comfort to us: "Lord, grant me the ability to accept the things I cannot change, the courage to change the things that can be changed, and the wisdom to know the difference."

In Closing

I moved away from St. Vincent's Home in 1963 to an apartment with Dad across town, although the emotional ties had not been severed. I remained connected by telephone calls, letters and visits to St. Vincent's and the girls I had grown up with.

Linda Saure helped fill the void of no longer living "sorority-style." She was the daughter of Dad's best friend, Phillip. Every five or six months, Phillip would return from his tour of duty with the Merchant Marines in the Mediteranean or the Pacific. Linda, Dad, Phillip and I would help spend his money, eating out at the finest restaurants in the city. Linda, home from college during the holidays and the summer, lived with us. She would spend, spend, spend, buying clothes like a fashion model, until her father got called away to the ship. Naturally, she needed someone to go shopping with, and I was right there when she wanted to discard her college-appropriate but barely used old clothing. Their timing felt perfectly synchronized. When Linda returned to Vermont for school, Phillip, broke but happy, seemed to hop his next ship.

Months before my graduation from St. Patrick's Academy, I treated myself to something I'd wanted for many years—contact lenses. Only the very wealthy or the very vain could buy them. After months of saving my paychecks from my summer job at the Sears, Roebuck & Company Credit Office, I had enough money to buy them.

Several months before graduation, I marched up to an office building at 14th and G Streets, took the elevator to the eye doctor's office, and paid my $150 for a pair of *Vent-Air Contact Lenses*, the state-of-the-arts new line of "hard" contact lenses. They advertised that the four vents on each lens allowed a better flow of oxygen to the eye, an improvement on the first edition of contact lenses. My nose and ears were always sore from the sheer weight of the Coke-bottle thick lenses. And I must have dropped and broken four or five frames over the years from cheerleading and playing softball. I was determined to never wear my "goggles" again.

I also began to experiment with makeup, especially eyeliner and mascara, determined to be live without the shield of glasses. And I wanted to be comfortable with both the lenses and the newly-painted face before graduation day. My vision seemed to clear again.

It took a long time for any joy and gaiety to enter our city, our school and our home after the death of John Kennedy. But eventually people moved on from the mourning and the loss.

From across the "Big Pond" came a bright spot. The Beatles came to America in February of 1964 and appeared on the Ed Sullivan Show. Beatlemania had hit. Everyone loved the four musicians from Liverpool, England. The Beatles seemed to breathe life back into the younger generation. It's true that "Imitation is the greatest form of flattery." Everyone donned the Beatle-like apparel. Everyone tried on the accent. Everyone cut their hair in a "shag" hairdo to look more like their British heroes. My hair was already in a shag because I had sold it to a wig shop downtown.

During my senior year, while living with my Dad in D.C., I went on a bus trip to Pennsylvania with the high school girls from St. Vincent's. It was a great opportunity for my vanity to burst forth—I could now brag about my new contact lenses and my freshly pierced ears. But more than just the socializing on the bus, we had a remarkable mission. We were on our way to see Inez Velasquez and Lani Vega in the convent in Pennsylvania. It seems they had gone full circle from their earlier school days with the same order of Sisters in Cuba to actually joining the order themselves. They could have become bitter women because of the situation with Fidel Castro's dictatorship in Cuba. Yet they chose to do the work of God through their religious vocations. We were so proud of them.

209

Four of my fellow St. Pat's alumnae and I bought round-trip bus tickets on Greyhound and visited the World's Fair a few days after our graduation. We left from the New York Avenue terminal and did a "poor man's tour" of the big city, visiting the Empire State Building, St. Patrick's, and Chinatown. Joan Landolt and I even ventured into Greenwich Village and picked up two "beatniks" in a coffee shop. We received the scorn of our fellow travelers when we got back to the hotel.

On the way back to D.C., boldly smoking El Producto cigars in the back seat of the Greyhound Bus, I secretly wished I were returning "home" to St. Vincent's. I missed the girls and the Sisters.

We had been given the Civil Service examination for "Clerk Stenographer" at school while still a junior at St. Patrick's Academy. A month before graduation I landed a Civil Service secretarial job at the United States Peace Corps Headquarters in Washington. The head of our department was Frank Manckiewiez; his boss was Sargent Shriver, head of the Peace Corps. Again I felt as though I were back into the arena with some of the beautiful people associated with John Kennedy's "Camelot." I was just one of the stenos but it was a great experience for a starry-eyed optimistic idealist in 1964!

Mr. Mankiewicz' office was on one floor; Mr. Shriver's was on another. They would take the steps and meet on the landings between floors to conduct business. They were both such approachable, down-to-earth people. Everyone at the Peace Corps seemed to have inherited a little piece of the Kennedy charismatic personality and style. This included my balmy Aunt Clara who was the elevator operator in our building at the Peace Corps. She'd brazenly flirt with Mr. Shriver. It was all in fun; he was a good sport. He would laugh and say, "Don't take your work so seriously." We were fulfilling John Kennedy's dream of worldwide peace through out day-to-day jobs.

In the years that followed, as each girl graduated from her respective high school she also moved away from St. Vincent's. Mary Elisabeth Holmes and some others remained at St. Vincent's to complete a year or two of college at Trinity College or Catholic

University. The girls moved on to take jobs in Washington or other areas, and most married and began having children.

The annual Ladies Auxiliary's famous Spaghetti Dinners had become the reunions for the alumnae. The networking continued by the women who had left St. Vincent's in the years before the mid-1960's.

In 1967 the Archdiocese of Washington made plans to relocate St. Vincent's with its smaller population of girls. The remaining girls were placed out into the community in good, local foster homes. With the invaluable help of several social workers from Catholic Charities—Sister Mary Blanche, then Superior of St. Vincent's; Sister Anne Joseph; Sister Frances Hill; Sister Frances McSherry—good foster homes "headed by a mother and a father" were meticulously chosen for the girls. The mothers were called "group mothers." Everything possible was done to assure that the girls would be well cared for.

Father Adler, Sister Dorothy and Sister Mary had a great deal to do with the logistics of the actual closing in 1968. They completed an inventory of the remaining equipment and other household goods, then offered any furnishings to the new group home families.

Sister Mary said, "It was felt that transferring these furnishings would not only give the families some of the best of everything available from St. Vincent's, but this action would also have the continuity of the work of St. Vincent's Home and bring the girls the familiarity and comfort from their former home."

When all of the furnishings had been distributed throughout the network of the various foster homes, the remaining items were placed in a "memorabilia room," a room which had previously served as the high school girls' study. An announcement was placed in the *Washington Post* that invited the alumnae of St. Vincent's to visit St. Vincent's one more time. They could choose furnishings or pieces of memorabilia to take home.

Selma Frank opted for her favorite lamp. Doris Burroughs took a statue of the Sacred Heart. Mary Elizabeth Lyons chose a recognizable sofa from the parlor. Years later her husband, Joshua Lyons jokingly referred to the sofa's style as "Early Orphan."

They took one last look at their home. Then the girls left St. Vincent's. The overhead lights went out for the last time.

Father Adler continued his morning jaunts to St. Vincent's—a daily habit that spanned 27 years. He wept when the building was destroyed. He eventually stopped his walks to the property where the hundreds of St. Vincent's girls, deeply saddened by the closing, spent their childhood. The wrecking ball was successful in demolishing the building. The memories lingered on.

Vignettes of a Rich Heritage

For you the reader, perhaps a lover of history, the best has been saved for last. The following are vignettes of the history of St. Vincent's Home and School and St. Rose's School.

St. Vincent's Orphan Asylum was incorporated by an Act of Congress and approved February 5, 1821. An institution like St. Vincent's had great prominence and promise, and was desperately needed in the City of Washington.

To know what else was occurring around 1821 is to understand the importance that was placed on an institution such as St. Vincent's.

In 1809, a New York native—Elizabeth Ann Bayley Seton— acquired land in Emmitsburg, began the work of the Sisters of Charity in the United States and initiated the first Catholic schools in America.

In 1821 the Union consisted of 12 free states and 12 slave states.

Seven years prior to St. Vincent's incorporation, within two miles of the site, the White House, Capitol and other government buildings were set on fire during the war against the British.

Native Americans were being pushed into shrinking territories.

Slavery was an issue that America had yet to confront.

Inflaming many on the subject of slavery, the novel *Uncle Tom's Cabin*, was printed in 1852.

Within 40 years of St. Vincent's incorporation, the United States was at war—a war against itself, where brother fought brother—the war between the North and the South.

Sister Serena Branson directed her dissertation to the Faculty of the National Catholic School of Social Service of the Catholic University of America in partial fulfillment of the requirements for the degree of Master of Social Work, "Two Child-Care Institutions Administered by the Sisters of Charity in the District of Columbia." These institutions were St. Vincent's Home and St. Rose's Technical School, later called St. Rose School. Sister Serena's paper included this history of St. Vincent's Home, with information from W. E. Smith, History of St. Patrick's Parish and from the Archives of St. Joseph's Central House, Emmitsburg, Maryland:

Less than half a century after the establishment of our nation, Saint Vincent's Asylum was founded. This institution was the second of its kind in Washington, antedated only by the Washington City Orphanage, now known as Hillcrest. In 1812 and 1817, Mother Seton's Sisters of Charity had gone to Philadelphia and New York to care for dependent children, and in 1825, at the request of the Reverend William Matthews, they opened their first house in the Nation's Capitol.

Father Matthews himself had come to Washington in 1804. His "restless energy, foresight, and zeal for the interest of Church and State" gave impetus to the prosperity of both St. Patrick's Parish and the Nation's Capitol. He has been truly called "the patriarch of Washington." Though pioneering for the Church in the Capitol City of a new nation and maintaining a spiritual guidance over a vast territory, Father Matthews found time to participate actively in the government of Georgetown College; to aid in the founding of Gonzaga College; to establish the nucleus of future parishes; and to begin work among the orphans. It is with his endeavors in this last field that we are particularly interested.

The Reverend William Matthews was the son of a well-known and well-to-do Maryland family. When but a youth he was sent to study at the English College in Liege, Belgium. His travels and social life seem not to have made him a lover of the material but rather to have developed a more intense zeal for using his material resources for the greater glory of God.

After his studies at St. Mary's College, Baltimore, which he entered upon his return from Belgium, he was ordained to the priesthood. He has the distinction of being the first native of the United States to be so elevated. This took place in 1800; and four years later, his energetic, ardent nature won for him the approval of Archbishop John Carroll, who bestowed on him the pastorate of St. Patrick's Parish, Washington, D.C. His persistent efforts to advance the Church within his parish territory led to the erection of a new church and rectory, to the establishment of a day school on F Street, later Gonzaga College, and to a complete spiritual uplifting of his congregation.

Father Matthews, as can be seen, was the spiritual leader of the Catholics of Washington. However, in spite of his many duties, he found time to devote to the little ones who had been deprived of the care of their parents, and in 1825 he determined to found an asylum where they would be under the tender guardianship of the good sisters. Possibly he may have, with his usual wonderful foresight, looked into the future and pictured the present magnificent building at Edgewood the outgrowth of the humble little orphanage he founded. We can scarecely imagine that he ever dreamed that in the far future it would dispose of its Tenth Street property for the princely sum of $450,000.

The sphere of the work of the Sisters of Charity of St. Joseph's, Emmitsburg, Maryland, appealed to Father Matthews, and he did not hesitate to address his appeal for aid to the little band so new and yet so staunch and firmly established. He therefore sent the following letter to Mother Rose White, Superioress of the Sisters of Charity:

> July 15, 1825
> Dear Sister:
>
> I have long wished to have a branch of your society established here; $400 are subscribed for this intention, to be paid for three years. A part of the first year's $400 is already deposited in the bank, and the whole will be paid in a few months. You will, therefore, be pleased to consider what three sisters you will, with the approbation for the Rev. Mr. Dubois, determine to send to this city. As Mr. Dubois is absent, I mention the subject to you, that you may have time to consider the subject maturely. When will he return? It will be well for him to come here and examine

what has been done. Be pleased to accept the little pictures
I send you, and pray for your humble servant.
    W. Matthews

It was due to this generous appeal that Sister Mary Augustine
Decount, Sister Clotilda Council and Sister Petronilla Smith were sent
to form the embryonic community of the new orphanage.

Father Matthews, after payment of his funeral expenses and other
incidentals, gave to the trustees of St. Vincent's Orphan Asylum
$5,000 of his 6 percent stock of the corporation of Washington, for
"the uses and purposes of the female department." He also gave the
remainder of his corporation of Washington stock, to go toward "the
purchase or erection of a male branch of said asylum," and if it were
not built within 5 years from the date of his death, it would be applied
to the uses and purposes of the female branch of the asylum.

President Abraham Lincoln had a special place in his heart for
widows and orphans. The following is from *The Collected Works of
Abraham Lincoln*, edited by Roy P. Basler, on the occasion of the
Proclamation of Thanksgiving, on November 21, 1864.

> I do therefore invite my fellow citizens in every part of
> the United States... to set apart and observe the last
> Thursday of November next, as a day of Thanksgiving
> and Praise to our beneficent Father who dwelleth in the
> Heavens. And I recommend to them that while offering
> up the ascriptions justly due to Him for such singular
> deliverances and blessings, they do also ... commend to
> His tender care all those who have become widows,
> orphans, mourners or sufferers in the lamantable civil
> strife in which we are unavoidably engaged, and fervently
> implore the interposition of the Almighty Hand to heal
> the wounds of the nation ... to the full enjoyment of peace,
> harmony, tranquility and Union.

Nestled in the rolling hills of northern Frederick County, Maryland
is the town of Emmitsburg where Elizabeth Ann Bayley founded the

order of the Sisters of Charity. The website of The National Shrine of St. Elizabeth Ann Seton, as well as the grounds and the entire complex appear to aid pilgrims to learn more about St. Elizabeth Ann Seton's life and good works. They provide the perfect reflective environment for seeking spiritual enlightenment and guidance.

Saint Elizabeth Ann Seton, from a prominent Episcopal family, was born on August 28, 1774 in New York City. Her life spanned the full spectrum of human experiences. She was a New York socialite, then became a devoted wife and mother of five children. She was dedicated to charitable organizations. Elizabeth Ann Seton—educator, social minister, catechist, spiritual leader and formator—was a tireless servant of God.

It was not until 1805 that she became a Roman Catholic. In March of 1809, she pronounced her vows before Bishop John Carroll of Baltimore and was given some property in Emmitsburg, Maryland. In June she began the organization that became "the American foundation of the Sisters of Charity of Emmitsburg."

The organization of the Sisters of Charity of St. Joseph's at Emmitsburg was the first new community for religious women to be established in the United States. She also began Saint Joseph's Academy and Free School, the first free Catholic School for girls staffed by Sisters in the United States.

"The legacy she left now includes six religious communities with more than 5,000 members, hundreds of schools, social service centers, and hospitals throught America and around the world."

She was canonized a saint in 1975 and had the distinction of being the first native-born North American to be canonized.

The early records of St. Vincent's Asylum register a personal contribution from President Abraham Lincoln and a donation from Andrew Jackson's Inaugural Ball.

It seems yet another President of the United States paid special attention to the work and welfare of St. Vincent's Asylum. The following is provided courtesy of the Archives, Daughters of of Charity, Emmitsburg, Maryland:

1849   (11-23-15-)

A New Asylum.

The building occupied by the Sisters in Washington belonged originally to Father Mathews. He had given it to the Jesuits, but he purchased it back from them for the Sisters' use, and there the Asylum was opened, and for over twenty years it served the double purpose of Asylum and School. The "Gonzaga Hall" of the present day is the old Asylum remodelled, the cradle of the Washington missions. In 1849 a new Asylum, long a necessity, was projected, and means being now at hand, foundations were cast. The following is a complete list of the articles deposited in the corner stone of Asylum laid May 14, 1849: Relics of St. Vincent, the cross and beads; pictures of our Lord and Blessed Mother, medals and pictures of different saints; a little one a prayer on beads, Catholic Almanac for 1849; a miniature figure of a Sister of Charity in full costume; a miniature figure of a female orphan in the uniform of the institution; names of the trustees of the Asylum, viz. Rev. William Mathews, Rev. J. Santarosa, Rev. James B. Donelan, Thos. Carbery and Wm. Hickey; names of the Lady Managers of the Asylum; viz. Mrs. Hoeman, Mrs. Fuller, Mrs. A. L. Slire, Mrs. E. A. Lee, Mrs. J. Graham, Mrs. Ferran, Mrs. Stubbs, Mrs. Clarke, and Mrs. Riggs; names of the Sisters and orphans then in the institution; an engraved likeness of Pius IX.; one of Archbp. Eccleston; one of Rev. Wm. Mathews; one of Gen. Taylor, President of the United States; epitaphs from the wills of Mathew Wright, James Cantwell, Elizabeth J. Green, James Sayton, who contributed to the support... & Col. Hickey, Father Hickey's brother...

to the support of St. Vincent's Orphan Asylum; a statistical table of the population of the United States, and each of the several States; an engraved likeness of the Rev. Louis R. Deluol, D.D., Superior of the Sisters of Charity, a medal of Gen. Washington, with the Washington National Monument on the reverse side; an engraving of the Washington National Monument, with several addresses from the Board of Managers; a list of the Managers of the Grand Inauguration Ball given to Gen. Taylor, March 5, 1849, with the letter of Robert Farnham, Esq., Treasurer, addressed to the Treasurer of St. Vincent's Orphan Asylum, enclosing $1,250, one half the net proceeds of the Ball, for the support of said Asylum; the names of the officers of the Corporation of Washington; the Charter of St. Vincent's Orphan Asylum, passed February 25, 1831, and signed Andrew Stevenson, Speaker of the House of Representatives, John C. Calhoun, Vice President, and Andrew Jackson, President of the United States; the names of the Sisters of Charity, and the first Lady Managers of the Institution; the Constitution of the United States, and statistics by Col. Wm Hickey; and a number of the Baltimore Sun.

Sister Mary de Sales Tyler who had been for more than two years at the head of the affairs of the Asylum, was still in place when this good work was commenced and completed. The new Asylum was on 10th Street, and was built on the site of house occupied previously by McClouth and School House known as "McClouth's School House."

The following brief history is contained in St. Vincent's Centennial 1925, a commemorative book compiled by the Reverend Dr. Stafford and others, on the occasion of St. Vincent's Centennial.

The Sisters came from St. Joseph's, Emmitsburg, Maryland for their new mission, Sister Mary Augustine Decount as "Sister Servant" and Sisters Clotilda Council and Petronilla Smith as "Assistants." They left St. Joseph's for Washington October 4, 1825.

Very few records of these days remain; the works were commenced apparently as little deeds scarcely worth record of notice. Sister Martha Daddisman, an authority in all that relates to old times, since she was one of Mother Seton's first companions, states that the Sisters were first 'located in a small house which stands back of F Street,' and the Sisters commenced with a Day School only. In the first year the orphans numbered about 30.

On July 18, 1832, Congress granted a donation of $20,000 worth of land, to be divided equally between St. Vincent's Orphan Asylum and the Washington City Asylum. The Washington City Asylum later became the boys' asylum. Seventy of these lots, valued at $10,000 in 1832, were scattered in various places around the District of Columbia.

On the feast of St. Anthony, June 13, 1899, the Old St. Vincent's ground on Tenth Street was sold by the Board of Directors for $450,000. A portion of the sum was used to purchase the Kate Chase Sprague residence, at Edgewood, which was considered north of the City at that time. On May 3, 1900, the ground was broken for a new home. On May 24th of the same month, a cornerstone was laid by his Eminence Cardinal Gibbons, in the presence of the faculty of the Catholic University of America, many priests from Baltimore and Washington, a number of sisters from various Religious houses of the City, and a large assemblage of the laity.

The work was pushed by the builder, John S. Larcombe, and the house was ready for occupancy December 18, 1900. The formal opening took place June 1, 1901. St Vincent's chapel was dedicated March 30, 1902. It is a memorial to R. O. Holzman.

There are now (1925) about 150 orphans in the Institution, ranging from seven to fourteen years of age. The school embraces all the grades from the lowest to the eighth grade. The large, well-lighted dormitories, like the rest of the house, are models of good housekeeping. In a word the house is in every respect a model institution, and reflects great credit on the Sisters of Charity, who show so much interest in the orphans God has given them to care for.

The Ladies of Charity were the first of the great foundations founded by St.Vincent de Paul. It was canonically erected on December 8, 1617, after having been approved by the Archbishop of Lyons. It has become an international organization with 450,000 members in 47 countries.

The National Organization consists of 47,000 members in 29 states. In 1960, the Ladies of Charity became an integrated unit of the national Conference of Catholic Charities. The first conference of the National Association of the Ladies of Charity was held in Atlantic City in September, 1962, and was attended by approximately 270 members. The Archdiocesan Council of the Ladies of Charity of Washington, D.C. has 1,100 members (1964).

In the Archdiocese of Washington, the Ladies of Charity have rendered a Spritualized Volunteer Service for more than quarter of a century (1964). Upon being invested as a Lady of Charity, she receives the "Image of the Son of God, Model of Charity." She recites an Act of Consecration in which she consecrates herself, under the auspices and according to the spirit of St. Vincent de Paul to the service of the poor whom for the future she considers her Master. "Through Thy bounty, Jesus, Thou hast placed us in the condition which will permit us to dry many tears, sweeten many sorrows and solace much suffering. With Thee and by Thee we desire to be dispensers of the spiritual and temporal treasures to our indigent and sufferent brothers."

To call a woman a "Lady of Charity" is to confer upon her one of the noblest titles that she can receive.

Knowing the intimate needs of the residents of St. Vincent's an Auxiliary was formed. This was in September 1920. With dues at a dollar a year, the nucleus of sixty had increased to more than a thousand members in two months. This devoted group furnished substantial help to carry out projects at St.Vincent's that could never be met from its ordinary revenue.

In a booklet on the occasion of the 1960 Annual Winter Card Party, given at the Catholic Daughters' Club House in Washington, D.C., the Very Reverend Monsignor Leo J. Coady, Director of Catholic Charities bragged about the Ladies of Charity.

> In my work around the archdiocese, I am often asked the question: 'Who are the Ladies of Charity?' ...what do they do?...there is so much that the Ladies of Charity do that I find I have a lengthy litany of activities that I could relate...at St. Vincent's Home, the Ladies of Charity perform a variety of useful works for the benefit of the children...tutoring...social activities....ready at any time to engage in any work of service that would help the Sisters in their great task of providing a true home for the girls....Ladies of Charity feel honored in being able to serve those in need...readiness to do for others for the sake of Christ...

On May 29, 1928, through an Act of Congress, St. Vincent's Orphan Asylum changed its name to "St. Vincent's Home and School." The Board of Trustees feared this name change would jeopardize bequests for the institution.

St. Vincent's Home and School was one of the original agencies that joined the of Community Chest in 1929, the first year of the Community Chest's formation. During the years prior to this, financial hardships were a constant source of anxiety to the Sisters. In that year St. Vincent's was the recipient of $24,090 or approximately 57 percent of its total annual income of $42,071.

The enthralling and extensive details of the history of Saint Rose School of Washington, D.C., 1868 to 1946, and its symbiotic relationship with St. Vincent's Home are briefly sketched here.

In 1868, the dual establishment, headed by Sister Blanche Rooney, comprised St. Vincent's Academy, a school for young ladies of the Nation's Capitol, and St. Vincent's Asylum, where children total or partially orphaned were cared for and taught in an institution separate from the academy. Father Walter, pastor of St. Patrick's and President of the Board of Trustees of St. Vincent's Asylum decided with Sister Blanche to discontinue placing children in families and to adopt some plan whereby they could remain in the institution. St. Rose's School of Industry took birth in a small room on the fourth floor of St. Vincent';s where three girls were initiated into the art of dressmaking, an occupation considered suitable employment for women.

This institution for girls over 14 years of age, continued to function at St. Vincent's until 1875 when a separate residence was built. In order to support themselves, the girls and Sisters made dresses at fifty cents apiece, started a small bakery where they sold rolls and cakes, and established a millinery shop. An addition was built in 1887. Further expansion required a new building, and in 1891 the Sisters purchased the site at California Street and Phelps Place, N. W. Through the generousity of a gentleman named Leach, they also acquired a summer home in Ocean City which was used for vacationing until 1908 for "relaxation and relief form the traditional heat of the Nation's Capitol."

In 1908, after a Congressional invesitigation, 55th Congress, and a re-emphasis of its mission, St Rose's Technical School was erected on the California Street property. Planned by Baltimore architect Francis E. Tormey, the building was considered one of the most up-to-date structures of this character in this country. Shortly after the Sisters and girls moved into their new residence, St. Rose's became "the parish of the delegation" with Monsignor Ceretti, then secretary to the Papal Delegate becoming the resident chaplain.

Prior to World War I the Sisters realized the retreating demand for the work of seamstresses, fitters and designers. The girls were then sent out to high schools in the city for business training. Classes in commercial work were provided at St. Rose's after the war. Providentially St. Rose's joined the Community Chest in 1929; this assistance was responsible for progress made in the 1930s and 1940s.

In 1936 the Sisters of Charity purchased property known as "Dutchman's Point" at Mayo, Maryland which served as the camp for the girls in the summer.

After studies were made in 1939 and 1941 by the Child Welfare League of America, St. Rose's was accredited by the Middle Atlantic

States Association of Colleges and Secondary Schools and affiliated with the Catholic University. In 1945 day student were admitted to classes and college preparatory classes were offered.

In January of 1946 St. Ann's Infant Home was condemned by the District inspectors for safety and health reasons, forcing the community of the Sisters of Charity to look for suitable quarters for the infant and maternity home. By March of 1946 a decision was reached to close St. Rose's as a home and school for dependent adolescents, and to turn the building over to St. Ann's until such time as it would be possible for that institution to build. The closing of St. Rose's was a cause of genuine sorrow to Sisters, students and members of the alumnae. The girls under care were discharged to relatives, placed in foster homes or transferred to St. Vincent's Home. Camp Saint Rose at Mayo, Maryland received the girls for a pleasant summer and in late August St. Vincent's received additional members who would live there while attending the various parochial high schools.

In 1975, Elizabeth Ann Bayley Seton, Foundress of the Sisters of Charity in the United States, was canonized in Saint Peter's Square by Pope Paul VI as the first American-born saint.

The following was extracted from the article *Edgewood: A History of the Residents* which was copyrighted by Mindy Glover in the year 2000.

> Only two other buildings have occupied the land at the intersection of 4th & Edgewood Street. In the mid 1800's Salmon P. Chase, an aid to President Abraham Lincoln, originally resided in the city at 601 E Street, N. W. However, after his daughter married a Senator from Rhode Island, they moved in and turned the city home into political salon. Around 1870, Chase built a country mansion on a hill overlooking the Glenwood cemetery, then naming it Edgewood and making it the first building to occupy what is now known as Edgewood Terrace.
>
> Kate Sprague, Chase's daughter, later moved into the mansion after being shunned from D.C. society for having

an extra-marital affair with the Senator from New York. Unable to support herself or pay for upkeep of the mansion, she began to sell chicken eggs. Additionally, she had sold off most of Edgewood's 50 acres before her death at the age of 58. With her passing, President McKinley sent Kate Sprague's body on a train back to Ohio and the house all but vanished without a trace.

The second structure built on the hill overlooking the U.S. Capitol to the south side and Catholic University to the north, was St. Vincent's Orphanage and Girls Home. St. Vincent's appeared on D.C. maps as early as 1936. Edgewood Street was then named Central Avenue. At this time, Baker & Ross Structural Steel and Government Warehouse buildings were all that stood between the Catholic Institution and Rhode Island Avenue.

In 1966 the District of Columbia, in order to meet low-income housing demands, zoned the land for construction of subsidized and market-rate housing. The Catholic Church made a decision to redirect its efforts and closed the doors of St. Vincent's Orphanage in 1968. Eugene Ford, a private developer from Bethesda, Maryland, purchased the land in 1970 and started the construction of 884 rental units spread out among mid and high-rise buildings along with garden apartments on the 16 acres of land. These buildings are what make up Edgewood Terrace today.

The Voices and Spirit of My Sisters

These are the voices and spirit of my childhood Sisters, and their experiences in living at our home, St. Vincent's, in Washington, D.C.

I tell my grandchildren about my growing up in an orphanage. They love to hear the stories.

"I owe a debt of gratitude to the good nuns that helped raise me. There were my family and instilled in me a strong religious belief and moral character. I have five children; they are the joy of my life.

God has truly blessed me with a perfect husband and children. I talk so much about the old days at St. Vincent's & St. Rose's that sometimes my husband teases me, calling me 'Sister Regina.' Sister Regina was a nun who first taught me to walk at St. Ann's where I lived before I went to St. Vincent's. I was named after Sister Regina.

—Regina Manelli DiGennaro

The following story is about Mary Alliata. The way she first arrived on the doorstep of St. Vincent's Home was typical of many of the girls' entrance before the days of social welfare intervention.

In 1939 seven-year-old Mary Alliata was left standing at the steps of the girls home with an empty shopping bag and two pennies and wearing a flowered dress. Alliata is only one of many girls who would come to live there over the next 30 years, and she is an example of the strong and long-lasting bonds that were built on this property. Mary Elizabeth Lyons, a childhood friend remembers Alliata as showing particular kindness to her. 'She has never asked anyone for anything, but she has given so much of herself.

The true strength of the familial connection formed at St. Vincent's Orphanage became apparent when Alliata's 57-year-old-body slowly began to deteriorate due to a deadly kidney disease. Three of her pals from her days at St. Vincent's held a benefit dinner to raise $30,000 in donations for Alliata so that she could receive a liver transplant. Shirtley Holt mailed 150 letters informing other St. Vincent friends of Alliata's illness. The women credit their generosity to growing up on the corner of 4th Street and Edgewood in Northeast Washington. 'You didn't think of yourself first; you thought of the next person. And when you do that growing up, you certainly don't stop when you leave the orphanage.

Now living in Baltimore, Maryland, Eva, remembers her days at St. Vincent's.

My two sisters and I were placed at St. Vincent's during the early 1940s. Our aunt, Sister Angela Heinekamp, had once been 'Sister Servant' at St. Vincent's When our mother's health failed, Sister Angela asked her superiors in Emmitsburg if we could stay in D.C. for a month. Sister Germaine Farrell was in charge there and welcomed us. Sister Germaine delighted in holding my youngest sister on her lap. Later my sister took 'Germaine' as her confirmation name.

World War II meant frequent air raid drills and no flood

lights were allowed to show of the dome of the Capitol. The dome of the Capitol was parallel to the attic level of St. Vincent's.
　—Eva Neidringhaus

I will always be grateful to the Daughters of Charity, especially Sister Alma, for her love and laughter. My youngest daughter is named 'Alma' in her honor. (This happens to be another one of the children of St. Vincent's alumnae named in Sister Alma's honor that I am aware of; perhaps there are several more women who named their daughters 'Alma.')

After such initial turmoil, I went on to a stable and happy adult life. I am a mother of three, a college graduate and a Registered Nurse, attributing much of this stability to the environment in which we lived at St. Vincent's. The Daughters of Charity provided structure, security and the values of their Catholic faith. They nurtured a love of music, books and God.
　—Stella Hill

These are some impressions about Father Adler, chaplain at St. Vincent's and the spirit of the Home.

He was a true father to one and all...what they lacked in parental environment and guidance, Father and the good Sisters of Charity made up for with lots of love and much spiritual guidance...St. Vincent's Home was one of a kind, perhaps unmatched today...there still exists a bond of loyalty...which will never be broken—a combination of affection, respect and togetherness which all families try to cultivate and keep over the years.
　—Doris Greiner Burroughs

My fondest memories are of Father Adler and the things he would make at Christmas and also throwing pennies in the pool. We would dive in the pool to get them...These were the best years of my life, especially the truck ride to

Camp St. Rose and once a week we would go to Beverly Beach for the day...my years at St. Vincent's taught me about the love and support the Sisters gave us to go out in the world to succeed...If ever I would win a lottery I would open up another home like St. Vicent's.
—Irene Connery Edwards

The happiness, sadness and joy of what we have from our experiences of just being part of that time with Father Adler and the good Sisters of Charity never can be taken away.
—Pat Prettyman Bailey

I'm 88 years old and can still remember everything that happened to me and my two sisters, Jeannie and Peggy who also lived at St. Vincent's. We had so many good times there.
We had nicknames for each of the Sisters. My favorite was 'Petsy' who was 'an angel in Angeltown.' Petsy was close to Fulton J. Sheen who used to come into our classroom to speak. Fulton J. Sheen would sometimes be accompanied by his many 'converts.'
I should have written a book myself but they'd never print all of my stories of mischief.
—Catherine DeForge Plummer

These thoughts were expressed by a former Superior of St. Vincent's in the 1960-era.

A squeezed hand and a kiss at night cures many a tear-stained pillow when you work with school-aged girls who feel unloved and let down by everyone.
—Sister Genevieve Simms

Doris Cecelia Burroughs summed up her feelings about St. Vincent's in this poem she wrote on the occasion of a reunion and celebration that honored four of the Daughters of Charity of St.

Vincent dePaul long after St. Vincent's had closed its doors. Cardinal Patrick A. O'Boyle and Bishop Thomas W. Lyons were among the nearly 150 guests who paid tribute to Sister Eliza Finnegan, Sister Serena Branson, Sister Mary Frank and Sister Mary Frances at a party at St. Ann's Infant and Maternity Home in Hyattsville, Maryland.

"Our Wonderful Moms, in your blue and white.
Even when 'campused,' we knew you were right..
The beautiful May Processions in the spring-time sun.
The swimming pool and parties and getting our chores done.
We'll love you always, we are proud to say.
For without your help, we might have lost the way.
Oh, what fun we had those many years gone by,
Our Memories so numerous and great, they'll never die.
You taught us to love and always respect others.
Thank Heavens, we had you as 'Our Mothers'...."

We shall not forget our early beginnings and the lessons in love for God through service to our fellow man manifested so generously by the Sisters of Charity of St. Vincent's Home and School. This is now my "Morning Prayer:"

Dear Lord, for the loving gift to us of Your servants Vincent and Elizabeth ,whose pioneering spirit brought us to You and to Your Word, we praise You.

St. Vincent de Paul, for the spirit of willing service to the poor that you brought to this world, we laud you.

Beloved St. Elizabeth Ann Seton for your bequest of loving and community sharing through sisterhood, we give you thanks.

Lord, remember the Daughters of Charity who unselfishly cared for us in our childhood,

And keep the daughters of the Daughters of Charity, with whom we shared our childhood, wherever they may be, safe and in the palm of Your Hand. Amen

Epilogue

Washington, D.C. has witnessed great transformations, shifting slowly from the "village" of my childhood with autonomous friendly little neighborhoods, to a great metropolitan city that competes with other international capitals in commerce and culture. Yet, the zones that segregate Washington—Northeast, Southeast, Northwest, Southwest—are the same dividing lines of economic and social factions that existed in the 1960s. Poverty, racial bias, class castes, greed, avarice and apathy still reside in the Nation's Capitol City.

The Catholic Church has been attacked in the 1990s and into the new millenium from every angle for what has been called its "tolerance" of hundreds of sexual abuse cases of children by parish priests. Incredible accusations and assumptions have been made about priests, their superiors and the Catholic Church as a whole. Regrettably, some may be true and justice will be served. At this writing, many legal cases are still outstanding and may not be resolved for some time. As a result, centuries of good works have been obscured.

Meanwhile Pope John Paul II has interceded to mend the damage from many of the sins of mankind's flawed history. He and the faithful work fervently toward world peace.

Changes have been made to our "old stomping grounds"—the

neighborhood between St. Vincent's Home and School and St. Anthony's Grade School. Modern, multi-plex housing units are in place for about a thousand people, replacing the 19-acre complex that was formerly St. Vincent's property once surrounded by a six-foot chain link fence. Now located in the original site of the Lourdes grotto is a huge blue painted sign—*THE PARKE*. Under this name is the name *VANTAGE at Edgewood Terrace*.

Holy Redeemer College and the Redemptorist home where Father Adler lived, remains intact on 7th Street. The DGS convenience store is now the Franklin Market & Liquor Store. Dickey's Dry Cleaners is now the Baptist Fellowship. College Pharmacy was replaced with the 7th Street Market, but is now boarded up. There is now a Metro subway station in the neighborhood at 4th and Rhode Island Avenue, Northeast.

The "circle house" at 10th Street and Irving is still lovingly maintained and landscaped. But alas, the Vander Vossen home at the other end of 10th Street near St. Anthony's, whose European-looking facade, was once the pride of the neighborhood, is overrun with weeds. The little painted wooden windmill and the layers and layers of tulips that graced the nooks and crannies of the yard are nowhere in sight.

The Brookland Hardware Store on the corner of 12th Street and Lawrence in the Brookland district is thriving. The old People's Drug Store that was in the middle of the block is closed and the old Newton Theatre at the corner was converted to a CVS store.

There is no trace of Torres Café, the beer joint that was located a few blocks from Union Station, where Mom "filled her tank" religiously in the 1960s. The fig tree at the house at South Carolina Avenue still stands but the figs look healthier at the Eastern Market just a few blocks away near Hine Junior High School. The old cinder-block Alsop home wears a new coat of pukie white paint and still sticks out like a sore thumb in lovely Georgetown. It's for sale.

Our "DC-centric vision" was broadened very soon after graduation from high school. While we once considered our hometown to be the center of the universe, we now view D.C. like most tourists and rarely visit for more than a few hours, never going beyond the boundaries of the S.W. Mall along the Tourmobile sightseeing route.

Union Station feels like the epicentre of tourism, with its shops and "turista traps" in and outside the building. Boarding a train there can still connect you with the rest of the continental United States, but most people view it as the hub for commuter rail service to Maryland, Virginia and West Virginia residences. We perceive the many bridges that cross the flowing Potomac River and link the many arteries around the City as merely additional barriers, blocking the flow of commuter traffic into the Nation's Capitol City.

So much for the infrastructure and the old haunts.

Our parents, godparents, aunt and uncle, all loved and missed deeply, have all passed away. Our Blessed Father Adler and most of the Sisters who cared for us at St. Vincent's have also passed away in the last several years.

The island country of Cuba is still under the dictatorship of Fidel Castro. Cuban nationals have become assimilated into the American community but many still hold hope that one day they can return to their beloved country.

As for the women who lived at St. Vincent's, the majority still live in the Washington, D.C. area. There are a handful—96 women to be exact —listed on a shrinking mailing list, thinned by notification of death or envelopes marked *Addressee Moved, left no forwarding address.*

There is is now an informal organization that produces a periodic newsletter in an attempt to have the women network with one another—the *Association of St. Vincent's and St. Rose's of Washington, D.C.* A reunion is planned every several years by the alumnae and a handful of former associates of St. Vincent's and Sisters who served there. This group is shrinking.

Sadly, the generation of women of the 1960 to 1968 era cannot be found. It is difficult to locate former residents. More than likely, most of these women married and changed their last names. Many women choose to remain outside of the network and we do respect that. We believe the central problem is the communication gap with the hundreds of women still alive who lived at St. Vincent's, is that the actual infrastructure of St. Vincent's no longer exists.

My husband Gene visits his hometown, Kitzmiller, Maryland, regularly and through homecomings, visits and telephone calls is able to maintain and nurture old friendships. We who lived at St. Vincent's are not able to do that. In so many ways, we are like "Orphans of the Wind," a phrase Gene uses to express the concept of not having control over your own destiny.

We have lost our physical homeplace. Moreover, we have lost our fundamental emotional roots. Families continue on, when an elderly loved one dies, through emotional and tangent bequests—shared stories from other family members, cherished photographs, a favorite piece of jewelry or some such heirloom.

The heirloom we did inherit is the priceless legacy left to us by the Daughters of Charity—the deep abiding love and faith in Our Lord Jesus Christ, and the commitment to serve others in His name. Our home, St. Vincent's Home and School, is no longer a place on a map. The memories of St. Vincent's are in a place deep within each of us, along with the diktat to live a life that embraces Jesus Christ. They are sheltered forever in our hearts.

References

The Association of St. Vincent's and St. Rose's of Washington, D.C., 1997-2004. Personal accounts from the alumnae. c/o 8989 Leetown Road, Kearneysville, WV 25435.

Branson, Sister Serena, *Two Child-Care Institutions administered by the Sisters of Charity in the District of Columbia.* Thesis for Master's Degree from Catholic University, 1946. Washington, D.C.

Conner, Kristina Heidler, N.D., University of Bridgeport, New Haven, Connecticut, *www.thehealingpowerofnature.com* 2004.

Glover, Mindy, *"Edgewood: A History of the Residents."* 2000. Washington, D.C.

"Insight Guide: CUBA," Insight Print Services, APA Publications, 1995, 1999, 2000. Singapore

Merry, Robert, *"Taking on the World: The Alsop Brothers."* 1996. Viking Press.

National Shrine of St. Elizabeth Ann Seton Website, www.emmitsburg.net/setonshrine/, Emmitsburg.

"One Hundred Twenty Five Years of St. Vincent's." 1925. Washington, D.C.

Reed Newland, Mary, *"The Saint Book."* New York. The Seabury Press, 1979.

Smith, Milton E., *History of St. Patrick's Parish.* 1904. Washington, D.C.

An aerial view of "the Home" circa 1955

The Daughters of Charity at St. Vincent's Home in the late 1950s.

REVEREND
EDWARD JOSEPH ADLER
C.SS.R.

BORN	—————— JUNE 6, 1899
PROFESSED	—————— AUGUST 2, 1919
ORDAINED	———— SEPTEMBER 14, 1924
DIED	—————— JANUARY 4, 1983

Father Adler – a father, a mentor, a friend.

Pauline Perello, an 8th grader, was chosen to be May
Queen in the annual May Procession at St. Vincent's

Jean Rose Woodhouse, on the Merry-Go-Round in "the Grove"

Check out another fascinating book of life in the 1950s and 1960s from the other end of the Potomac River. Read *Orphans of the Wind* by G.M. Smith, PublishAmerica.

Printed in the United States
24478LVS00005B/1-27